ON CONSOLATION

TO HELVIA AND TO MARCIA

SENECA

Translated by
AUBREY STEWART

Cover by: Filibooks Covers

Published by: Fili Public

Filibooks ApS

info@filibooks.com

CVR: 37100161

Paperback ISBN: 978-87-94559-20-1
Ebook ISBN: 978-87-94559-21-8

CONTENTS

TO HELVIA

TO MARCIA

TO HELVIA

1

I

My best of mothers, I have often felt eager to console you, and have as often checked that impulse. Many things urged me to make the attempt: in the first place, I thought that if, though I might not be able to restrain your tears, yet that if I could even wipe them away, I should set myself free from all my own sorrows: then I was quite sure that I should rouse you from your grief with more authority if I had first shaken it off myself. I feared, too, lest fortune, though overcome by me, might nevertheless overcome someone of my family. Then I endeavoured to crawl and bind up your wounds in the best way I could, holding my hand over my own wound; but then again other considerations occurred to me which held me back: I knew that I must not oppose your grief during its first transports, lest my very attempts at consolation might irritate it, and add fuel to it: for in diseases, also, there is nothing more hurtful than medicine applied too soon. I waited, therefore, until it exhausted itself by its own violence, and being weakened by time, so that it was able to bear remedies, would allow itself to be handled and touched. Beside this, while turning over all the works which the greatest geniuses have composed, for the purpose of soothing and pacifying grief, I could not find any instance of one who had offered consolation to his relatives, while he himself was being sorrowed over by them. Thus, the subject being a new one, I hesitated and feared that instead of consoling, I might embitter your grief. Then here was the thought that a man who had only just raised his head after burying his child, and who wished to console his friends, would require to use new phrases not taken from our common everyday words of comfort: but every sorrow of more than usual magnitude must needs prevent one's choosing one's words, seeing that it often prevents one's using one's very voice. However this may be, I will make the attempt, not trusting in my own genius, but because my consolation will be most powerful since it is I who offer it. You never would deny me anything, and I hope, though all grief is obstinate, that you will surely not refuse me this request, that you will allow me to set bounds to your sorrow.

2

II

See how far I have presumed upon your indulgence: I have no doubts about my having more power over you than your grief, than which nothing has more power over the unhappy. In order, therefore, to avoid encountering it straightaway, I will at first take its part and offer it every encouragement: I will rip up and bring to light again wounds already scarred. Someone may say, "What sort of consolation is this, for a man to rake up buried evils, and to bring all its sorrows before a mind which scarcely can bear the sight of one?" but let him reflect that diseases which are so malignant that they do but gather strength from ordinary remedies, may often be cured by the opposite treatment: I will, therefore, display before your grief all its woes and miseries: this will be to effect a cure, not by soothing measures, but by cautery and the knife. What shall I gain by this? I shall make the mind that could overcome so many sorrows, ashamed to bewail one wound more in a body so full of scars. Let those whose feeble minds have been enervated by a long period of happiness, weep and lament for many days, and faint away on receiving the slightest blow: but those whose years have all been passed amid catastrophes should bear the severest losses with brave and unyielding patience. Continual misfortune has this one advantage, that it ends by rendering callous those whom it is always scourging. Ill fortune has given you no respite, and has not left even your birthday free from the bitterest grief: you lost your mother as soon as you were born, nay, while you were being born, and you came into life, as it were, an outcast: you grew up under a stepmother, whom you made into a mother by all the obedience and respect which even a real daughter could have bestowed upon her: and even a good stepmother costs everyone dear. You lost your most affectionate uncle, a brave and excellent man, just when you were awaiting his return: and, lest fortune should weaken its blows by dividing them, within a month you lost your beloved husband, by whom you had become the mother of three children. This sorrowful news was brought you while you were already in mourning, while all your children were absent, so that all your misfortunes seemed to have been purposely brought upon you at a time when your grief could nowhere find any repose. I pass over all the dangers and alarms which you have endured without any respite: it was but the other day that you received the bones of three of your grandchildren in the bosom from which you had sent them forth: less than twenty days after you had buried my child, who perished in your arms and amid your kisses, you heard that I had been exiled: you wanted only this drop in your cup, to have to weep for those who still lived.

3

III

The last wound is, I admit, the severest that you have ever yet sustained: it has not merely torn the skin, but has pierced you to the very heart: yet as recruits cry aloud when only slightly wounded, and shudder more at the hands of the surgeon than at the sword, while veterans even when transfixed allow their hurts to be dressed without a groan, and as patiently as if they were in someone else's body, so now you ought to offer yourself courageously to be healed. Lay aside lamentations and wailings, and all the usual noisy manifestations of female sorrow: you have gained nothing by so many misfortunes, if you have not learned how to suffer. Now, do I seem not to have spared you? nay, I have not passed over any of your sorrows, but have placed them all together in a mass before you.

4

———

IV

I have done this by way of a heroic remedy: for I have determined to conquer this grief of yours, not merely to limit it; and I shall conquer it, I believe, if in the first place I can prove that I am not suffering enough to entitle me to be called unhappy, let alone to justify me in rendering my family unhappy: and, secondly, if I can deal with your case and prove that even your misfortune, which comes upon you entirely through me, is not a severe one. The point to which I shall first address myself is that of which your motherly love longs to hear, I mean, that I am not suffering: if I can, I will make it clear to you that the events by which you think that I am overwhelmed, are not unendurable: if you cannot believe this, I at any rate shall be all the more pleased with myself for being happy under circumstances which could make most men miserable. You need not believe what others say about me: that you may not be puzzled by any uncertainty as to what to think, I distinctly tell you that I am not miserable: I will add, for your greater comfort, that it is not possible for me to be made miserable.

$$\frac{5}{V}$$

We are born to a comfortable position enough, if we do not afterwards lose it: the aim of Nature has been to enable us to live well without needing a vast apparatus to enable us to do so: every man is able by himself to make himself happy. External circumstances have very little importance either for good or for evil: the wise man is neither elated by prosperity nor depressed by adversity; for he has always endeavoured to depend chiefly upon himself and to derive all his joys from himself. Do I, then, call myself a wise man? far from it: for were I able to profess myself wise, I should not only say that I was not unhappy, but should avow myself to be the most fortunate of men, and to be raised almost to the level of a god: as it is, I have applied myself to the society of wise men, which suffices to lighten all sorrows, and, not being as yet able to rely upon my own strength, I have betaken myself for refuge to the camp of others, of those, namely, who can easily defend both themselves and their friends. They have ordered me always to stand as it were on guard, and to mark the attacks and charges of Fortune long before she delivers them; she is only terrible to those whom she catches unawares; he who is always looking out for her assault, easily sustains it: for so also an invasion of the enemy overthrows those by whom it is unexpected, but those who have prepared themselves for the coming war before it broke out, stand in their ranks fully equipped and repel with ease the first, which is always the most furious onset. I never have trusted in Fortune, even when she seemed most peaceful. I have accepted all the gifts of wealth, high office, and influence, which she has so bountifully bestowed upon me, in such a manner that she can take them back again without disturbing me: I have kept a great distance between them and myself: and therefore she has taken them, not painfully torn them away from me. No man loses anything by the frowns of Fortune unless he has been deceived by her smiles: those who have enjoyed her bounty as though it were their own heritage forever, and who have chosen to take precedence of others because of it, lie in abject sorrow when her unreal and fleeting delights forsake their empty childish minds, that know nothing about solid pleasure: but he who has not been puffed up by success, does not collapse after failure: he possesses a mind of tried constancy, superior to the influences of either state; for even in the midst of prosperity he has experimented upon his powers of enduring adversity. Consequently I have always believed that there was no real good in any of those things which all men desire: I then found that they were empty, and merely painted over with artificial and deceitful dyes, without containing anything within which corresponds to their outside: I now find nothing so harsh and fearful as the common opinion of mankind threatened me with in this which is known as adversity: the word itself, owing to the prevalent belief and ideas current about it, strikes somewhat unpleasantly upon one's ears, and thrills the hearers as something dismal and accursed, for so hath the vulgar decreed that it should be: but a great many of the decrees of the vulgar are reversed by the wise.

6

VI

Setting aside, then, the verdict of the majority, who are carried away by the first appearance of things and the usual opinion about them, let us consider what is meant by exile: clearly a changing from one place to another. That I may not seem to be narrowing its force, and taking away its worst parts, I must add, that this changing of place is accompanied by poverty, disgrace, and contempt. Against these I will combat later on: meanwhile I wish to consider what there is unpleasant in the mere act of changing one's place of abode. "It is unbearable," men say, "to lose one's native land." Look, I pray you, on these vast crowds, for whom all the countless roofs of Rome can scarcely find shelter: the greater part of those crowds have lost their native land: they have flocked hither from their country towns and colonies, and in fine from all parts of the world. Some have been brought by ambition, some by the exigencies of public office, some by being entrusted with embassies, some by luxury which seeks a convenient spot, rich in vices, for its exercise, some by their wish for a liberal education, others by a wish to see the public shows. Some have been led hither by friendship, some by industry, which finds here a wide field for the display of its powers. Some have brought their beauty for sale, some their eloquence: people of every kind assemble themselves together in Rome, which sets a high price both upon virtues and vices. Bid them all to be summoned to answer to their names, and ask each one from what home he has come: you will find that the greater part of them have left their own abodes, and journeyed to a city which, though great and beauteous beyond all others, is nevertheless not their own. Then leave this city, which may be said to be the common property of all men, and visit all other towns: there is not one of them which does not contain a large proportion of aliens. Pass away from those whose delightful situation and convenient position attracts many settlers: examine wildernesses and the most rugged islands, Sciathus and Seriphus, Gyarus and Corsica: you will find no place of exile where someone does not dwell for his own pleasure. What can be found barer or more precipitous on every side than this rock? what more barren in respect of food? what more uncouth in its inhabitants? more mountainous in its configuration? or more rigorous in its climate? yet even here there are more strangers than natives. So far, therefore, is the mere change of place from being irksome, that even this place has allured some away from their country. I find some writers who declare that mankind has a natural itch for change of abode and alteration of domicile: for the mind of man is wandering and unquiet; it never stands still, but spreads itself abroad and sends forth its thoughts into all regions, known or unknown; being nomadic, impatient of repose, and loving novelty beyond everything else. You need not be surprised at this, if you reflect upon its original source: it is not formed from the same elements as the heavy and earthly body, but from heavenly spirit: now heavenly things are by their nature always in motion, speeding along and flying with the greatest swiftness. Look at the luminaries which light the world: none of them stands still. The sun is perpetually in motion, and passes from one quarter to another, and although he revolves with the entire heaven, yet nevertheless he has a motion in the contrary direction to that of the universe itself, and passes through all the constellations without remaining in any: his wandering is incessant, and he never ceases to move from place to place. All things continually revolve and are forever changing; they pass from one position to another in accordance with natural and unalterable laws: after they have completed a certain circuit in a fixed space of time, they begin again the path which they had previously trodden. Be not surprised, then, if the human mind, which is formed from the same seeds as the heavenly bodies, delights in change and wandering, since the divine nature itself either takes pleasure in constant and exceeding swift motion or perhaps even preserves its existence thereby.

VII

Come now, turn from divine to human affairs: you will see that whole tribes and nations have changed their abodes. What is the meaning of Greek cities in the midst of barbarous districts? or of the Macedonian language existing among the Indians and the Persians? Scythia and all that region which swarms with wild and uncivilized tribes boasts nevertheless Achaean cities along the shores of the Black Sea. Neither the rigours of eternal winter, nor the character of men as savage as their climate, has prevented people migrating thither. There is a mass of Athenians in Asia Minor. Miletus has sent out into various parts of the world citizens enough to populate seventy-five cities. That whole coast of Italy which is washed by the Lower Sea is a part of what once was "Greater Greece." Asia claims the Tuscans as her own: there are Tyrians living in Africa, Carthaginians in Spain; Greeks have pushed in among the Gauls, and Gauls among the Greeks. The Pyrenees have proved no barrier to the Germans: human caprice makes its way through pathless and unknown regions: men drag along with them their children, their wives, and their aged and worn-out parents. Some have been tossed hither and thither by long wanderings, until they have become too wearied to choose an abode, but have settled in whatever place was nearest to them: others have made themselves masters of foreign countries by force of arms: some nations while making for parts unknown have been swallowed up by the sea: some have established themselves in the place in which they were originally stranded by utter destitution. Nor have all men had the same reasons for leaving their country and for seeking for a new one: some have escaped from their cities when destroyed by hostile armies, and having lost their own lands have been thrust upon those of others: some have been cast out by domestic quarrels: some have been driven forth in consequence of an excess of population, in order to relieve the pressure at home: some have been forced to leave by pestilence, or frequent earthquakes, or some unbearable defects of a barren soil: some have been seduced by the fame of a fertile and overpraised clime. Different people have been led away from their homes by different causes; but in all cases it is clear that nothing remains in the same place in which it was born: the movement of the human race is perpetual: in this vast world some changes take place daily. The foundations of new cities are laid, new names of nations arise, while the former ones die out, or become absorbed by more powerful ones. And yet what else are all these general migrations but the banishments of whole peoples? Why should I lead you through all these details? what is the use of mentioning Antenor the founder of Padua, or Evander who established his kingdom of Arcadian settlers on the banks of the Tiber? or Diomedes and the other heroes, both victors and vanquished, whom the Trojan war scattered over lands which were not their own?

It is a fact that the Roman Empire itself traces its origin back to an exile as its founder, who, fleeing from his country after its conquest, with what few relics he had saved from the wreck, had been brought to Italy by hard necessity and fear of his conqueror, which bade him seek distant lands. Since then, how many colonies has this people sent forth into every province? wherever the Roman conquers, there he dwells. These migrations always found people eager to take part in them, and veteran soldiers desert their native hearths and follow the flag of the colonists across the sea. The matter does not need illustrations by any more examples: yet I will add one more which I have before my eyes: this very island[1] has often changed its inhabitants. Not to mention more ancient events, which have become obscure from their antiquity, the Greeks who inhabit Marseilles at the present day, when they left Phocaea, first settled here, and it is doubtful what drove them hence, whether it was the rigour of the climate, the sight of the more powerful land of Italy, or the want of harbours on the coast: for the fact of their having placed themselves in the midst of what were then the most savage and uncouth tribes of Gaul proves that they were not driven hence by the ferocity of the natives. Subsequently the Ligurians came over into this same island, and also the Spaniards,[2] which is proved by the resemblance of their customs: for they wear the same head-coverings and the same sort of shoes as the Cantabrians, and some of their words are the same: for by association with Greeks and Ligurians they have entirely lost their native speech. Hither since then have been brought two Roman colonies, one by Marius, the other by Sulla: so often has the population of this barren and thorny rock been changed. In fine, you will scarcely find any land which is still in the hands of its original inhabitants: all peoples have become confused and intermingled: one has come after another: one has wished for what another scorned: some have been driven out of the land which they took from another. Thus fate has decreed that nothing should ever enjoy an uninterrupted course of good fortune.

8

VIII

Varro, that most learned of all the Romans, thought that for the mere change of place, apart from the other evils attendant on exile, we may find a sufficient remedy in the thought that wherever we go we always have the same Nature to deal with. Marcus Brutus thought that there was sufficient comfort in the thought that those who go into exile are permitted to carry their virtues thither with them. Though one might think that neither of these alone were able to console an exile, yet it must be confessed that when combined they have great power: for how very little it is that we lose! whithersoever we betake ourselves two most excellent things will accompany us, namely, a common Nature and our own especial virtue. Believe me, this is the work of whoever was the Creator of the universe, whether he be an all-powerful deity, an incorporeal mind which effects vast works, a divine spirit by which all things from the greatest to the smallest are equally pervaded, or fate and an unalterable connected sequence of events, this, I say, is its work, that nothing above the very lowest can ever fall into the power of another: all that is best for a man's enjoyment lies beyond human power, and can neither be bestowed or taken away: this world, the greatest and the most beautiful of Nature's productions, and its noblest part, a mind which can behold and admire it, are our own property, and will remain with us as long as we ourselves endure. Let us therefore briskly and cheerfully hasten with undaunted steps whithersoever circumstances call us: let us wander over whatever countries we please; no place of banishment can be found in the whole world in which man cannot find a home. I can raise my eyes from the earth to the sky in one place as well as in another; the heavenly bodies are everywhere equally near to mankind: accordingly, as long as my eyes are not deprived of that spectacle of which they never can have their fill, as long as I am allowed to gaze on the sun and moon, to dwell upon the other stars, to speculate upon their risings and settings, their periods, and the reasons why they move faster or slower, to see so many stars glittering throughout the night, some fixed, some not moving in a wide orbit but revolving in their own proper track, some suddenly diverging from it, some dazzling our eyes by a fiery blaze as though they were falling, or flying along drawing after them a long trail of brilliant light: while I am permitted to commune with these, and to hold intercourse, as far as a human being may, with all the company of heaven, while I can raise my spirit aloft to view its kindred sparks above, what does it matter upon what soil I tread?

IX

"But this country does not produce beautiful or fruit-bearing trees; it is not watered by the courses of large or navigable rivers; it bears nothing which other nations would covet, since its produce barely suffices to support its inhabitants: no precious marbles are quarried here, no veins of gold and silver are dug out." What of that! It must be a narrow mind that takes pleasure in things of the Earth: it ought to be turned away from them to the contemplation of those which can be seen everywhere, which are equally brilliant everywhere: we ought to reflect, also, that these vulgar matters by a mistaken perversion of ideas prevent really good things reaching us: the further men stretch out their porticos, the higher they raise their towers, the more widely they extend their streets, the deeper they sink their retreats from the heats of summer, the more ponderous the roofs with which they cover their banqueting halls, the more there will be to obstruct their view of heaven. Fortune has cast you into a country in which there is no lodging more splendid than a cottage: you must indeed have a poor spirit, and one which seeks low sources of consolation, if you endure this bravely because you have seen the cottage of Romulus: say, rather, "Should that lowly barn be entered by the virtues, it will straightaway become more beautiful than any temple, because within it will be seen justice, self-restraint, prudence, love, a right division of all duties, a knowledge of all things on Earth and in heaven. No place can be narrow, if it contains such a company of the greatest virtues; no exile can be irksome in which one can be attended by these companions." Brutus, in the book which he wrote upon virtue, says that he saw Marcellus in exile at Mytilene, living as happily as it is permitted to man to live, and never keener in his pursuit of literature than at that time. He consequently adds the reflection: "I seemed rather to be going into exile myself when I had to return without him, than to be leaving him in exile." O how much more fortunate was Marcellus at that time, when Brutus praised him for his exile, than when Rome praised him for his consulship! what a man that must have been who made anyone think himself exiled because he was leaving him in exile! what a man that must have been who attracted the admiration of one whom even his friend Cato admired! Brutus goes on to say:— "Gaius Caesar sailed past Mytilene without landing, because he could not bear to see a fallen man." The Senate did indeed obtain his recall by public petition, being so anxious and sorrowful the while, that you would have thought that they all were of Brutus's mind that day, and were not pleading the cause of Marcellus, but their own, that they might not be sent into exile by being deprived of him: yet he gained far greater glory on the day when Brutus could not bear to leave him in exile, and Caesar could not bear to see him: for each of them bore witness to his worth: Brutus grieved, and Caesar blushed at going home without

Marcellus. Can you doubt that so great a man as Marcellus frequently encouraged himself to endure his exile patiently in some such terms as these: "The loss of your country is no misery to you: you have so steeped yourself in philosophic lore, as to know that all the world is the wise man's country? What! was not this very man who banished you absent from his country for ten successive years? he was, no doubt, engaged in the extension of the empire, but for all that he was absent from his country. Now see how his presence is required in Africa, which threatens to rekindle the war, in Spain which is nursing up again the strength of the broken and shattered opposite faction, in treacherous Egypt, in fine, in all the parts of the world, for all are watching their opportunity to seize the empire at a disadvantage. Which will he go to meet first? which part of the universal conspiracy will he first oppose? His victory will drag him through every country in the world. Let nations look up to him and worship him: do thou live satisfied with the admiration of Brutus."

10

X

Marcellus, then, nobly endured his exile, and his change of place made no change in his mind, even though it was accompanied by poverty, in which every man who has not fallen into the madness of avarice and luxury, which upset all our ideas, sees no harm. Indeed, how very little is required to keep a man alive? and who, that has any virtue whatever, will find this fail him? As for myself, I do not feel that I have lost my wealth, but my occupation: the wants of the body are few: it wants protection from the cold, and the means of allaying hunger and thirst: all desires beyond these are vices, not necessities. There is no need for prying into all the depths of the sea, for loading one's stomach with heaps of slaughtered animals, or for tearing up shellfish[1] from the unknown shore of the furthest sea: may the gods and goddesses bring ruin upon those whose luxury transcends the bounds of an empire which is already perilously wide. They want to have their ostentatious kitchens supplied with game from the other side of the Phasis, and though Rome has not yet obtained satisfaction from the Parthians, they are not ashamed to obtain birds from them: they bring together from all regions everything, known or unknown, to tempt their fastidious palate: food, which their stomach, worn out with delicacies, can scarcely retain, is brought from the most distant ocean: they vomit that they may eat, and eat that they may vomit, and do not even deign to digest the banquets which they ransack the globe to obtain. If a man despises these things, what harm can poverty do him? If he desires them, then poverty even does him good, for he is cured in spite of himself, and though he will not receive remedies even upon compulsion, yet while he is unable to fulfill his wishes he is as though he had them not. Gaius Caesar, whom in my opinion Nature produced in order to show what unlimited vice would be capable of when combined with unlimited power, dined one day at a cost of ten millions of sesterces: and though in this he had the assistance of the intelligence of all his subjects, yet he could hardly find how to make one dinner out of the tribute-money of three provinces. How unhappy are they whose appetite can only be aroused by costly food! and the costliness of food depends not upon its delightful flavour and sweetness of taste, but upon its rarity and the difficulty of procuring it: otherwise, if they chose to return to their sound senses, what need would they have of so many arts which minister to the stomach? of so great a commerce? of such ravaging of forests? of such ransacking of the depths of the sea? Food is to be found everywhere, and has been placed by Nature in every part the world, but they pass it by as though they were blind, and wander through all countries, cross the seas, and excite at a great cost the hunger which they might allay at a small one. One would like to say: Why do you launch ships? why do you arm your hands for battle both with men and wild beasts? why do you run so riotously hither and thither? why do you amass fortune after fortune? Are you unwilling to remember how small our bodies are? is it not frenzy and the wildest insanity to wish for so much when you can contain so little? Though you may increase your income, and extend the boundaries of your property, yet you never can enlarge your own bodies: when your business transactions have turned out well, when you have made a successful campaign, when you have collected the food for which you have hunted through all lands, you will have no place in which to bestow all these superfluities. Why do you strive to obtain so much? Do you think that our ancestors, whose virtue supports our vices even to the present day, were unhappy, though they dressed their food with their own hands, though the earth was their bed, though their roofs did not yet glitter with gold, nor their temples with precious stones? and so they used then to swear with scrupulous honesty by earthenware gods; those who called these gods to witness would go back to the enemy for certain death rather than break their word.[2] Do you suppose that our dictator who granted an audience to the ambassadors of the Samnites, while he roasted the commonest food before the fire himself with that very hand with which he had so often smitten the enemy, and with which he had placed his laurel wreath upon the lap of Capitolian Jove, enjoyed life less than the Apicius who lived in our own days, whose habits tainted the entire century, who set himself up as a professor of gastronomy in that very city from which philosophers once were banished as corrupters of youth? It is worthwhile to know his end. After he had spent a hundred millions of sesterces on his kitchen, and had wasted on each single banquet a sum equal to so many presents from the reigning emperors, and the vast revenue which he drew from the Capitol being overburdened with debt, he then for the first time was forced to examine his accounts: he calculated that he would have ten millions left of his fortune, and, as though he would live a life of mere starvation on ten millions, put an end to his life by poison. How great must the luxury of that man have been, to whom ten millions signified want? Can you think after this that the amount of money necessary to make a fortune depends upon its actual extent rather than on the mind of the owner? Here was a man who shuddered at the thought of a fortune of ten million sesterces, and escaped by poison from a prospect which other men pray for. Yet, for a mind so diseased, that last draught of his was the most wholesome: he was really eating and drinking poisons when he was not only enjoying, but boasting of his enormous banquets, when he was flaunting his vices, when he was causing his country to follow his example, when he was inviting youths to imitate him, albeit youth is quick to learn evil, without being provided with a model to copy. This is what befalls those who do not use their wealth according to reason, which has fixed limits, but according to vicious fashion, whose caprices are boundless and immeasurable. Nothing is sufficient for covetous desire, but Nature can be satisfied even with scant measure. The poverty of an exile, therefore, causes no inconvenience, for no place of exile is so barren as not to produce what is abundantly sufficient to support a man.

11

———

XI

Next, need an exile regret his former dress and house? If he only wishes for these things because of their use to him, he will want neither roof nor garment, for it takes as little to cover the body as it does to feed it: Nature has annexed no difficult conditions to anything which man is obliged to do. If, however, he sighs for a purple robe steeped in floods of dye, interwoven with threads of gold and with many coloured artistic embroideries, then his poverty is his own fault, not that of fortune: even though you restored to him all that he has lost, you would do him no good; for he would have more unsatisfied ambitions, if restored, than he had unsatisfied wants when he was an exile. If he longs for furniture glittering with silver vases, plate which boasts the signature of antique artists, bronze which the mania of a small clique has rendered costly, slaves enough to crowd however large a house, purposely overfed horses, and precious stones of all countries: whatever collections he may make of these, he never will satisfy his insatiable appetite, any more than any amount of liquor will quench a thirst which arises not from the need of drink but from the burning heat within a man; for this is not thirst but disease. Nor does this take place only with regard to money and food, but every want which is caused by vice and not by necessity is of this nature: however much you supply it with you do not quench it but intensify it. He who restrains himself within the limits prescribed by nature, will not feel poverty; he who exceeds them will always be poor, however great his wealth may be. Even a place of exile suffices to provide one with necessaries; whole kingdoms do not suffice to provide one with superfluities. It is the mind which makes men rich: this it is that accompanies them into exile, and in the most savage wildernesses, after having found sufficient sustenance for the body, enjoys its own overflowing resources: the mind has no more connection with money than the immortal gods have with those things which are so highly valued by untutored intellects, sunk in the bondage of the flesh. Gems, gold, silver, and vast polished round tables are but earthly dross, which cannot be loved by a pure mind that is mindful of whence it came, is unblemished by sin, and which, when released from the body, will straightaway soar aloft to the highest heaven: meanwhile, as far as it is permitted by the hindrances of its mortal limbs and this heavy clog of the body by which it is surrounded, it examines divine things with swift and airy thought. From this it follows that no free-born man, who is akin to the gods, and fit for any world and any age, can ever be in exile: for his thoughts are directed to all the heavens and to all times past and future: this trumpery body, the prison and fetter of the spirit, may be tossed to this place or to that; upon it tortures, robberies, and diseases may work their will: but the spirit itself is holy and eternal, and upon it no one can lay hands.

XII

That you may not suppose that I merely use the maxims of the philosophers to disparage the evils of poverty, which no one finds terrible, unless he thinks it so; consider in the first place how many more poor people there are than rich, and yet you will not find that they are sadder or more anxious than the rich: nay, I am not sure that they are not happier, because they have fewer things to distract their minds. From these poor men, who often are not unhappy at their poverty, let us pass to the rich. How many occasions there are on which they are just like poor men! When they are on a journey their baggage is cut down, whenever they are obliged to travel fast their train of attendants is dismissed. When they are serving in the army, how small a part of their property can they have with them, since camp discipline forbids superfluities! Nor is it only temporary exigencies or desert places that put them on the same level as poor men: they have some days on which they become sick of their riches, dine reclining on the ground, put away all their gold and silver plate, and use earthenware. Madmen! they are always afraid of this for which they sometimes wish. O how dense a stupidity, how great an ignorance of the truth they show when they flee from this thing and yet amuse themselves by playing with it! Whenever I look back to the great examples of antiquity, I feel ashamed to seek consolation for my poverty, now that luxury has advanced so far in the present age, that the allowance of an exile is larger than the inheritance of the princes of old. It is well known that Homer had one slave, that Plato had three, and that Zeno, who first taught the stern and masculine doctrine of the Stoics, had none: yet could anyone say that they lived wretchedly without himself being thought a most pitiable wretch by all men? Menenius Agrippa, by whose mediation the patricians and plebeians were reconciled, was buried by public subscription. Attilius Regulus, while he was engaged in scattering the Carthaginians in Africa, wrote to the Senate that his hired servant had left him, and that consequently his farm was deserted: whereupon it was decreed that as long as Regulus was absent, it should be cultivated at the expense of the State. Was it not worth his while to have no slave, if thereby he obtained the Roman people for his farm-bailiff? Scipio's daughters received their dowries from the Treasury, because their father had left them none: by Hercules, it was right for the Roman people to pay tribute to Scipio for once, since he had exacted it forever from Carthage. O how happy were those girls' husbands, who had the Roman people for their father-in-law. Can you think that those whose daughters dance in the ballet, and marry with a settlement of a million sesterces, are happier than Scipio, whose children received their dowry of old-fashioned brass money from their guardian the Senate? Can anyone despise poverty, when she has such a noble descent to boast of? can an exile be angry at any privation, when Scipio could not afford a portion for his daughters, Regulus could not afford a hired labourer, Menenius could not afford a funeral? when all these men's wants were supplied in a manner which rendered them a source of additional honour? Poverty, when such men as these plead its cause, is not only harmless, but positively attractive.

XIII

To this one may answer: "Why do you thus ingeniously divide what can indeed be endured if taken singly, but which all together are overwhelming? Change of place can be borne if nothing more than one's place be changed: poverty can be borne if it be without disgrace, which is enough to cow our spirits by itself." If anyone were to endeavour to frighten me with the number of my misfortunes, I should answer him as follows: If you have enough strength to resist any one part of your ill fortune, you will have enough to resist it all. If virtue has once hardened your mind, it renders it impervious to blows from any quarter: if avarice, that greatest pest of the human race, has left it, you will not be troubled by ambition: if you regard the end of your days not as a punishment, but as an ordinance of nature, no fear of anything else will dare to enter the breast which has cast out the fear of death. If you consider sexual passion to have been bestowed on mankind not for the sake of pleasure, but for the continuance of the race, all other desires will pass harmlessly by one who is safe even from this secret plague, implanted in our very bosoms. Reason does not conquer vices one by one, but all together: if reason is defeated, it is utterly defeated once for all. Do you suppose that any wise man, who relies entirely upon himself, who has set himself free from the ideas of the common herd, can be wrought upon by disgrace? A disgraceful death is worse even than disgrace: yet Socrates bore the same expression of countenance with which he had rebuked thirty tyrants, when he entered the prison and thereby took away the infamous character of the place; for the place which contained Socrates could not be regarded as a prison. Was anyone ever so blind to the truth as to suppose that Marcus Cato was disgraced by his double defeat in his candidature for the praetorship and the consulship? that disgrace fell on the praetorship and consulship which Cato honoured by his candidature. No one is despised by others unless he be previously despised by himself: a grovelling and abject mind may fall an easy prey to such contempt: but he who stands up against the most cruel misfortunes, and overcomes those evils by which others would have been crushed—such a man, I say, turns his misfortunes into badges of honour, because we are so constituted as to admire nothing so much as a man who bears adversity bravely. At Athens, when Aristides was being led to execution, everyone who met him cast down his eyes and groaned, as though not merely a just man but justice herself was being put to death. Yet one man was found who spat in his face: he might have been disturbed at this, since he knew it could only be a foul-mouthed fellow that would have the heart to do so; he, however, wiped his face, and with a smile asked the magistrate who accompanied him to warn that man not to open his mouth so rudely again. To act thus was to treat contumely itself with contempt. I know that some say that there is nothing more terrible than disgrace, and that they would prefer death. To such men I answer that even exile is often accompanied by no disgrace whatever: if a great man falls, he remains a great man after his fall, you can no more suppose that he is disgraced than when people tread upon the walls of a ruined temple, which the pious treat with as much respect as when they were standing.

14

—————

XIV

Since, then, my dearest mother, you have no reason for endless weeping on my account, it follows that your tears must flow on your own: there are two causes for this, either your having lost my protection, or your not being able to bear the mere fact of separation. The first of these I shall only touch upon lightly, for I know that your heart loves nothing belonging to your children except themselves. Let other mothers look to that, who make use of their sons' authority with a woman's passion, who are ambitious through their sons because they cannot bear office themselves, who spend their sons' inheritance, and yet are eager to inherit it, and who weary their sons by lending their eloquence to others: you have always rejoiced exceedingly in the successes of your sons, and have made no use of them whatever: you have always set bounds to our generosity, although you set none to your own: you, while a minor under the power of the head of the family, still used to make presents to your wealthy sons: you managed our inheritances with as much care as if you were working for your own, yet refrained from touching them as scrupulously as if they belonged to strangers: you have spared to use our influence, as though you enjoyed other means of your own, and you have taken no part in the public offices to which we have been elected beyond rejoicing in our success and paying our expenses: your indulgence has never been tainted by any thought of profit, and you cannot regret the loss of your son for a reason which never had any weight with you before his exile.

15

———

XV

All my powers of consolation must be directed to the other point, the true source of your maternal grief. You say, "I am deprived of the embraces of my darling son, I cannot enjoy the pleasure of seeing him and of hearing him talk. Where is he at whose sight I used to smooth my troubled brow, in whose keeping I used to deposit all my cares? Where is his conversation, of which I never could have enough? his studies, in which I used to take part with more than a woman's eagerness, with more than a mother's familiarity? Where are our meetings? The boyish delight which he always showed at the sight of his mother?" To all this you add the actual places of our merry-makings and conversation, and, what must needs have more power to move you than anything else, the traces of our late social life, for fortune treated you with the additional cruelty of allowing you to depart on the very third day before my ruin, without a trace of anxiety, and not fearing anything of the kind. It was well that we had been separated by a vast distance: it was well that an absence of some years had prepared you to bear this blow: you came home, not to take any pleasure in your son, but to get rid of the habit of longing for him. Had you been absent long before, you would have borne it more bravely, as the very length of your absence would have moderated your longing to see me: had you never gone away, you would at any rate have gained one last advantage in seeing your son for two days longer: as it was, cruel Fate so arranged it that you were not present with me during my good fortune, and yet have not become accustomed to my absence. But the harder these things are to bear, the more virtue you must summon to your aid, and the more bravely you must struggle as it were with an enemy whom you know well, and whom you have already often conquered. This blood did not flow from a body previously unhurt: you have been struck through the scar of an old wound.

XVI

You have no grounds for excusing yourself on the ground of being a woman, who has a sort of right to weep without restraint, though not without limit. For this reason our ancestors allotted a space of ten months' mourning for women who had lost their husbands, thus settling the violence of a woman's grief by a public ordinance. They did not forbid them to mourn, but they set limits to their grief: for while it is a foolish weakness to give way to endless grief when you lose one of those dearest to you, yet it shows an unnatural hardness of heart to express no grief at all: the best middle course between affection and hard common sense is both to feel regret and to restrain it. You need not look at certain women whose sorrow, when once begun, has been ended only by death: you know some who after the loss of their sons have never laid aside the garb of mourning: you are constitutionally stronger than these, and from you more is required. You cannot avail yourself of the excuse of being a woman, for you have no womanish vices. Unchastity, the greatest evil of the age, has never classed you with the majority of women; you have not been tempted either by gems or by pearls; riches have not allured you into thinking them the greatest blessing that man can own; respectably brought up as you were in an old-fashioned and strict household, you have never been led astray by that imitation of others which is so full of danger even to virtuous women. You have never been ashamed of your fruitfulness as though it were a reproach to your youth: you never concealed the signs of pregnancy as though it were an unbecoming burden, nor did you ever destroy your expected child within your womb after the fashion of many other women, whose attractions are to be found in their beauty alone. You never defiled your face with paints or cosmetics: you never liked clothes which showed the figure as plainly as though it were naked: your sole ornament has been a consummate loveliness which no time can impair, your greatest glory has been your modesty. You cannot, therefore, plead your womanhood as an excuse for your grief, because your virtues have raised you above it: you ought to be as superior to womanish tears as you are to womanish vices. Even women would not allow you to pine away after receiving this blow, but would bid you quickly and calmly go through the necessary amount of mourning, and then to arise and shake it off: I mean, if you are willing to take as your models those women whose eminent virtue has given them a place among even great men. Misfortune reduced the number of Cornelia's children from twelve to two: if you count the number of their deaths, Cornelia had lost ten: if you weigh them, she had lost the Gracchi: nevertheless, when her friends were weeping around her and using too bitter imprecations against her fate, she forbade them to blame fortune for having deprived[1] her of her sons the Gracchi. Such ought to have been the mother of him who, when speaking in the forum, said, "Would you speak evil of the mother who bore me?" The mother's speech seems to me to show a far greater spirit: the son set a high value on the birth of the Gracchi; the mother set an equal value on their deaths. Rutilia followed her son Cotta into exile, and was so passionately attached to him that she could bear exile better than absence from him; nor did she return home before her son did so: after he had been restored, and had been raised to honour in the republic, she bore his death as bravely as she had borne his exile. No one saw any traces of tears upon her cheeks after she had buried her son: she displayed her courage when he was banished, her wisdom when he died: she allowed no considerations either to interfere with her affection, or to force her to protract a useless and foolish mourning. These are the women with whom I wish you to be numbered: you have the best reasons for restraining and suppressing your sorrow as they did, because you have always imitated their lives.

17

XVII

I am aware that this is a matter which is not in our power, and that none of the passions, least of all that which arises from grief, are obedient to our wishes; indeed, it is overbearing and obstinate, and stubbornly rejects all remedies: we sometimes wish to crush it, and to swallow our emotion, but, nevertheless, tears flow over our carefully arranged and made-up countenance. Sometimes we occupy our minds with public spectacles and shows of gladiators; but during the very sights by which it is amused, the mind is wrung by slight touches of sorrow. It is better, therefore, to conquer it than to cheat it; for a grief which has been deceived and driven away either by pleasure or by business rises again, and its period of rest does but give it strength for a more terrible attack; but a grief which has been conquered by reason is appeased forever. I shall not, then, give you the advice which so many, I know, adopt, that you should distract your thoughts by a long journey, or amuse them by a beautiful one; that you should spend much of your time in the careful examination of accounts, and the management of your estate, and that you should keep constantly engaging in new enterprises: all these things avail but little, and do not cure, but merely obstruct our sorrow. I had rather it should be brought to an end than that it should be cheated: and, therefore, I would fain lead you to the study of philosophy, the true place of refuge for all those who are flying from the cruelty of Fortune: this will heal your wounds and take away all your sadness: to this you would now have to apply yourself, even though you had never done so before; but as far as my father's old-fashioned strictness permitted, you have gained a superficial, though not a thorough knowledge of all liberal studies. Would that my father, most excellent man that he was, had been less devoted to the customs of our ancestors, and had been willing to have you thoroughly instructed in the elements of philosophy, instead of receiving a mere smattering of it! I should not now need to be providing you with the means of struggling against Fortune, but you would offer them to me: but he did not allow you to pursue your studies far, because some women use literature to teach them luxury instead of wisdom. Still, thanks to your keen intellectual appetite, you learned more than one could have expected in the time: you laid the foundations of all good learning: now return to them: they will render you safe, they will console you, and charm you. If once they have thoroughly entered into your mind, grief, anxiety, the distress of vain suffering will never gain admittance thither: your breast will not be open to any of these; against all other vices it has long been closed. Philosophy is your most trustworthy guardian, and it alone can save you from the attacks of Fortune.

18

XVIII

Since, however, you require something to lean upon until you can reach that haven of rest which philosophy offers to you, I wish in the meantime to point out to you the consolations which you have. Look at my two brothers—while they are safe, you have no grounds for complaint against Fortune; you can derive pleasure from the virtues of each of them, different as they are; the one has gained high office by attention to business, the other has philosophically despised it. Rejoice in the great place of one of your sons, in the peaceful retirement of the other, in the filial affection of both. I know my brothers' most secret motives: the one adorns his high office in order to confer lustre upon you, the other has withdrawn from the world into his life of quiet, and contemplation, that he may have full enjoyment of your society. Fortune has consulted both your safety and your pleasure in her disposal of your two sons: you may be protected by the authority of the one, and delighted by the literary leisure of the other. They will vie with one another in dutiful affection to you, and the loss of one son will be supplied by the love of two others. I can confidently promise that you will find nothing wanting in your sons except their number. Now, then, turn your eyes from them to your grandchildren; to Marcus, that most engaging child, whose sight no sorrow can withstand. No grief can be so great or so fresh in anyone's bosom as not to be charmed away by his presence. Where are the tears which his joyousness could not dry? whose heart is so nipped by sorrow that his animation would not cause it to dilate? who would not be rendered mirthful by his playfulness? who would not be attracted and made to forget his gloomy thoughts by that prattle to which no one can ever be weary of listening? I pray the gods that he may survive us: may all the cruelty of fate exhaust itself on me and go no further; may all the sorrow destined for my mother and my grandmother fall upon me; but let all the rest flourish as they do now: I shall make no complaints about my childlessness or my exile, if only my sacrifice may be received as a sufficient atonement, and my family suffer nothing more. Hold in your bosom Novatilla, who soon will present you with great-grandchildren, she whom I had so entirely adopted and made my own, that, now that she has lost me, she seems like an orphan, even though her father is alive. Love her for my sake as well as for her own: Fortune has lately deprived her of her mother: your affection will be able to prevent her really feeling the loss of the mother whom she mourns. Take this opportunity of forming and strengthening her principles; nothing sinks so deeply into the mind as the teaching which we receive in our earliest years; let her become accustomed to hearing your discourses; let her character be moulded according to your pleasure: she will gain much even if you give her nothing more than your example. This continually recurring duty will be a remedy in itself: for when your mind is full of maternal sorrow, nothing can distract it from its grief except either philosophic argument or honourable work. I should count your father among your greatest consolations, were he not absent: as it is, judge from your affection for me what his affection is for you, and then you will see how much more just it is that you should be preserved for him than that you should be sacrificed to me. Whenever your keenest paroxysms of grief assail you and bid you give way to them, think of your father. By giving him so many grandchildren and great-grandchildren you have made yourself no longer his only daughter; but you alone can crown his prosperous life by a happy end: as long as he is alive it is impiety for you to regret having been born.

19

XIX

I have hitherto said nothing of your chief source of consolation, your sister, that most faithful heart which shares all your sorrows as fully as your own, and who feels for all of us like a mother. With her you have mingled your tears, on her bosom you have tasted your first repose: she always feels for your troubles, and when I am in the case she does not grieve for you alone. It was in her arms that I was carried into Rome: by her affectionate and motherly nursing I regained my strength after a long period of sickness: she enlarged her influence to obtain the office of quaestor for me, and her fondness for me made her conquer a shyness which at other times made her shrink from speaking to, or loudly greeting her friends. Neither her retired mode of life, nor her country-bred modesty, at a time when so many women display such boldness of manner, her placidity, nor her habits of solitary seclusion prevented her from becoming actually ambitious on my account. Here, my dearest mother, is a source from which you may gain true consolation: join yourself, as far as you are able, to her, bind yourself to her by the closest embraces. Those who are in sorrow are wont to flee from those who are dearest to them, and to seek liberty for the indulgence of their grief: do you let her share your every thought: if you wish to nurse your grief, she will be your companion, if you wish to lay it aside she will bring it to an end. If, however, I rightly understand the wisdom of that most perfect woman, she will not suffer you to waste your life in unprofitable mourning, and will tell you what happened in her own instance, which I myself witnessed. During a sea-voyage she lost a beloved husband, my uncle, whom she married when a maiden; she endured at the same time grief for him and fear for herself, and at last, though shipwrecked, nevertheless rescued his body from the vanquished tempest. How many noble deeds are unknown to fame! If only she had had the simple-minded ancients to admire her virtues, how many brilliant intellects would have vied with one another in singing the praises of a wife who forgot the weakness of her sex, forgot the perils of the sea, which terrify even the boldest, exposed herself to death in order to lay him in the earth, and who was so eager to give him decent burial that she cared nothing about whether she shared it or no. All the poets have made the wife[1] famous who gave herself to death instead of her husband: my aunt did more when she risked her life in order to give her husband a tomb: it shows greater love to endure the same peril for a less important end. After this, no one need wonder that for sixteen years, during which her husband governed the province of Egypt, she was never beheld in public, never admitted any of the natives to her house, never begged any favour of her husband, and never allowed anyone to beg one of her. Thus it came to pass that a gossiping province, ingenious in inventing scandal about its rulers, in which even the blameless often incurred disgrace, respected her as a singular example of uprightness,[2] never made free with her name—a remarkable piece of self-restraint among a people who will risk everything rather than forego a jest—and that at the present time it hopes for another governor's wife like her, although it has no reasonable expectation of ever seeing one. It would have been greatly to her credit if the province had approved her conduct for a space of sixteen years: it was much more creditable to her that it knew not of her existence. I do not remind you of this in order to celebrate her praises, for to take such scanty notice of them is to curtail them, but in order that you may understand the magnanimity of a woman who has not yielded either to ambition or to avarice, those twin attendants and scourges of authority, who, when her ship was disabled and her own death was impending, was not restrained by fear from keeping fast hold of her husband's dead body, and who sought not how to escape from the wreck, but how to carry him out of it with her. You must now show a virtue equal to hers, recall your mind from grief, and take care that no one may think that you are sorry that you have borne a son.

XX

However, since it is necessary, whatever you do, that your thoughts should sometimes revert to me, and that I should now be present to your mind more often than your other children, not because they are less dear to you, but because it is natural to lay one's hands more often upon a place that pains one; learn how you are to think of me: I am as joyous and cheerful as in my best days: indeed these days are my best, because my mind is relieved from all pressure of business and is at leisure to attend to its own affairs, and at one time amuses itself with lighter studies, at another eagerly presses its inquiries into its own nature and that of the universe: first it considers the countries of the world and their position: then the character of the sea which flows between them, and the alternate ebbings and flowings of its tides; next it investigates all the terrors which hang between heaven and earth, the region which is torn asunder by thunderings, lightnings, gusts of wind, vapour, showers of snow and hail. Finally, having traversed every one of the realms below, it soars to the highest heaven, enjoys the noblest of all spectacles, that of things divine, and, remembering itself to be eternal, reviews all that has been and all that will be forever and ever.

TO MARCIA

1

I

Did I not know, Marcia, that you have as little of a woman's weakness of mind as of her other vices, and that your life was regarded as a pattern of antique virtue, I should not have dared to combat your grief, which is one that many men fondly nurse and embrace, nor should I have conceived the hope of persuading you to hold fortune blameless, having to plead for her at such an unfavorable time, before so partial a judge, and against such an odious charge. I derive confidence, however, from the proved strength of your mind, and your virtue, which has been proved by a severe test. All men know how well you behaved towards your father, whom you loved as dearly as your children in all respects, save that you did not wish him to survive you: indeed, for all that I know you may have wished that also: for great affection ventures to break some of the golden rules of life. You did all that lay in your power to avert the death of your father, Aulus Cremutius Cordus;[1] but when it became clear that, surrounded as he was by the myrmidons of Sejanus, there was no other way of escape from slavery, you did not indeed approve of his resolution, but gave up all attempts to oppose it; you shed tears openly, and choked down your sobs, yet did not screen them behind a smiling face; and you did all this in the present century, when not to be unnatural towards one's parents is considered the height of filial affection. When the changes of our times gave you an opportunity, you restored to the use of man that genius of your father for which he had suffered, and made him in real truth immortal by publishing as an eternal memorial of him those books which that bravest of men had written with his own blood. You have done a great service to Roman literature: a large part of Cordus's books had been burned; a great service to posterity, who will receive a true account of events, which cost its author so dear; and a great service to himself, whose memory flourishes and ever will flourish, as long as men set any value upon the facts of Roman history, as long as anyone lives who wishes to review the deeds of our fathers, to know what a true Roman was like—one who still remained unconquered when all other necks were broken in to receive the yoke of Sejanus, one who was free in every thought, feeling, and act. By Hercules, the state would have sustained a great loss if you had not brought him forth from the oblivion to which his two splendid qualities, eloquence and independence, had consigned him: he is now read, is popular, is received into men's hands and bosoms, and fears no old age: but as for those who butchered him, before long men will cease to speak even of their crimes, the only things by which they are remembered. This greatness of mind in you has forbidden me to take into consideration your sex or your face, still clouded by the sorrow by which so many years ago it was suddenly overcast. See; I shall do nothing underhand, nor try to steal away your sorrows: I have reminded you of old hurts, and to prove that your present wound may be healed, I have shown you the scar of one which was equally severe. Let others use soft measures and caresses; I have determined to do battle with your grief, and I will dry those weary and exhausted eyes, which already, to tell you the truth, are weeping more from habit than from sorrow. I will effect this cure, if possible, with your goodwill: if you disapprove of my efforts, or dislike them, then you must continue to hug and fondle the grief which you have adopted as the survivor of your son. What, I pray you, is to be the end of it? All means have been tried in vain: the consolations of your friends, who are weary of offering them, and the influence of great men who are related to you: literature, a taste which your father enjoyed and which you have inherited from him, now finds your ears closed, and affords you but a futile consolation, which scarcely engages your thoughts for a moment. Even time itself, nature's greatest remedy, which quiets the most bitter grief, loses its power with you alone. Three years have already passed, and still your grief has lost none of its first poignancy, but renews and strengthens itself day by day, and has now dwelt so long with you that it has acquired a domicile in your mind, and actually thinks that it would be base to leave it. All vices sink into our whole being, if we do not crush them before they gain a footing; and in like manner these sad, pitiable, and discordant feelings end by feeding upon their own bitterness, until the unhappy mind takes a sort of morbid delight in grief. I should have liked, therefore, to have attempted to effect this cure in the earliest stages of the disorder, before its force was fully developed; it might have been checked by milder remedies, but now that it has been confirmed by time it cannot be beaten without a hard struggle. In like manner, wounds heal easily when the blood is fresh upon them: they can then be cleared out and brought to the surface, and admit of being probed by the finger: when disease has turned them into malignant ulcers, their cure is more difficult. I cannot now influence so strong a grief by polite and mild measures: it must be broken down by force.

II

I am aware that all who wish to give anyone advice begin with precepts, and end with examples: but it is sometimes useful to alter this fashion, for we must deal differently with different people. Some are guided by reason, others must be confronted with authority and the names of celebrated persons, whose brilliancy dazzles their mind and destroys their power of free judgment. I will place before your eyes two of the greatest examples belonging to your sex and your century: one, that of a woman who allowed herself to be entirely carried away by grief; the other, one who, though afflicted by a like misfortune, and an even greater loss, yet did not allow her sorrows to reign over her for a very long time, but quickly restored her mind to its accustomed frame. Octavia and Livia, the former Augustus's sister, the latter his wife, both lost their sons when they were young men, and when they were certain of succeeding to the throne. Octavia lost Marcellus, whom both his father-in-law and his uncle had begun to depend upon, and to place upon his shoulders the weight of the empire—a young man of keen intelligence and firm character, frugal and moderate in his desires to an extent which deserved especial admiration in one so young and so wealthy, strong to endure labour, averse to indulgence, and able to bear whatever burden his uncle might choose to lay, or I may say to pile upon his shoulders. Augustus had well chosen him as a foundation, for he would not have given way under any weight, however excessive. His mother never ceased to weep and sob during her whole life, never endured to listen to wholesome advice, never even allowed her thoughts to be diverted from her sorrow. She remained during her whole life just as she was during the funeral, with all the strength of her mind intently fixed upon one subject. I do not say that she lacked the courage to shake off her grief, but she refused to be comforted, thought that it would be a second bereavement to lose her tears, and would not have any portrait of her darling son, nor allow any allusion to be made to him. She hated all mothers, and raged against Livia with especial fury, because it seemed as though the brilliant prospect once in store for her own child was now transferred to Livia's son. Passing all her days in darkened rooms and alone, not conversing even with her brother, she refused to accept the poems which were composed in memory of Marcellus, and all the other honours paid him by literature, and closed her ears against all consolation. She lived buried and hidden from view, neglecting her accustomed duties, and actually angry with the excessive splendour of her brother's prosperity, in which she shared. Though surrounded by her children and grandchildren, she would not lay aside her mourning garb, though by retaining it she seemed to put a slight upon all her relations, in thinking herself bereaved in spite of their being alive.

3

III

Livia lost her son Drusus, who would have been a great emperor, and was already a great general: he had marched far into Germany, and had planted the Roman standards in places where the very existence of the Romans was hardly known. He died on the march, his very foes treating him with respect, observing a reciprocal truce, and not having the heart to wish for what would do them most service. In addition to his dying thus in his country's service, great sorrow for him was expressed by the citizens, the provinces, and the whole of Italy, through which his corpse was attended by the people of the free towns and colonies, who poured out to perform the last sad offices to him, till it reached Rome in a procession which resembled a triumph. His mother was not permitted to receive his last kiss and gather the last fond words from his dying lips: she followed the relics of her Drusus on their long journey, though every one of the funeral pyres with which all Italy was glowing seemed to renew her grief, as though she had lost him so many times. When, however, she at last laid him in the tomb, she left her sorrow there with him, and grieved no more than was becoming to a Caesar or due to a son. She did not cease to make frequent mention of the name of her Drusus, to set up his portrait in all places, both public and private, and to speak of him and listen while others spoke of him with the greatest pleasure: she lived with his memory; which none can embrace and consort with who has made it painful to himself.[1]Choose, therefore, which of these two examples you think the more commendable: if you prefer to follow the former, you will remove yourself from the number of the living; you will shun the sight both of other people's children and of your own, and even of him whose loss you deplore; you will be looked upon by mothers as an omen of evil; you will refuse to take part in honourable, permissible pleasures, thinking them unbecoming for one so afflicted; you will be loath to linger above ground, and will be especially angry with your age, because it will not straightaway bring your life abruptly to an end. I here put the best construction on what is really most contemptible and foreign to your character. I mean that you will show yourself unwilling to live, and unable to die. If, on the other hand, showing a milder and better regulated spirit, you try to follow the example of the latter most exalted lady, you will not be in misery, nor will you wear your life out with suffering. Plague on it! what madness this is, to punish oneself because one is unfortunate, and not to lessen, but to increase one's ills! You ought to display, in this matter also, that decent behaviour and modesty which has characterised all your life: for there is such a thing as self-restraint in grief also. You will show more respect for the youth himself, who well deserves that it should make you glad to speak and think of him, if you make him able to meet his mother with a cheerful countenance, even as he was wont to do when alive.

IV

I will not invite you to practise the sterner kind of maxims, nor bid you bear the lot of humanity with more than human philosophy; neither will I attempt to dry a mother's eyes on the very day of her son's burial. I will appear with you before an arbitrator: the matter upon which we shall join issue is, whether grief ought to be deep or unceasing. I doubt not that you will prefer the example of Julia Augusta, who was your intimate friend: she invites you to follow her method: she, in her first paroxysm, when grief is especially keen and hard to bear, betook herself for consolation to Areus, her husband's teacher in philosophy, and declared that this did her much good; more good than the thought of the Roman people, whom she was unwilling to sadden by her mourning; more than Augustus, who, staggering under the loss of one of his two chief supporters, ought not to be yet more bowed down by the sorrow of his relatives; more even than her son Tiberius, whose affection during that untimely burial of one for whom whole nations wept made her feel that she had only lost one member of her family. This was, I imagine, his introduction to and grounding in philosophy of a woman peculiarly tenacious of her own opinion:—"Even to the present day, Julia, as far as I can tell—and I was your husband's constant companion, and knew not only what all men were allowed to know, but all the most secret thoughts of your hearts—you have been careful that no one should find anything to blame in your conduct; not only in matters of importance, but even in trifles you have taken pains to do nothing which you could wish common fame, that most frank judge of the acts of princes, to overlook. Nothing, I think, is more admirable than that those who are in high places should pardon many shortcomings in others, and have to ask it for none of their own. So also in this matter of mourning you ought to act up to your maxim of doing nothing which you could wish undone, or done otherwise.

5

———————

V

"In the next place, I pray and beseech you not to be self-willed and beyond the management of your friends. You must be aware that none of them know how to behave, whether to mention Drusus in your presence or not, as they neither wish to wrong a noble youth by forgetting him nor to hurt you by speaking of him. When we leave you and assemble together by ourselves, we talk freely about his sayings and doings, treating them with the respect which they deserve: in your presence deep silence is observed about him, and thus you lose that greatest of pleasures, the hearing the praises of your son, which I doubt not you would be willing to hand down to all future ages, had you the means of so doing, even at the cost of your own life. Wherefore endure to listen to, nay, encourage conversation of which he is the subject, and let your ears be open to the name and memory of your son. You ought not to consider this painful, like those who in such a case think that part of their misfortune consists in listening to consolation. As it is, you have altogether run into the other extreme, and, forgetting the better aspects of your lot, look only upon its worse side: you pay no attention to the pleasure you have had in your son's society and your joyful meetings with him, the sweet caresses of his babyhood, the progress of his education: you fix all your attention upon that last scene of all: and to this, as though it were not shocking enough, you add every horror you can. Do not, I implore you, take a perverse pride in appearing the most unhappy of women: and reflect also that there is no great credit in behaving bravely in times of prosperity, when life glides easily with a favouring current: neither does a calm sea and fair wind display the art of the pilot: some foul weather is wanted to prove his courage. Like him, then, do not give way, but rather plant yourself firmly, and endure whatever burden may fall upon you from above; scared though you may have been at the first roar of the tempest. There is nothing that fastens such a reproach[1] on Fortune as resignation." After this he points out to her the son who is yet alive: he points out grandchildren from the lost one.

VI

It is your trouble, Marcia, which has been dealt with here: it is beside your couch of mourning that Areus has been sitting: change the characters, and it is you whom he has been consoling. But, on the other hand, Marcia, suppose that you have sustained a greater loss than ever mother did before you: see, I am not soothing you or making light of your misfortune: if fate can be overcome by tears, let us bring tears to bear upon it: let every day be passed in mourning, every night be spent in sorrow instead of sleep: let your breast be torn by your own hands, your very face attacked by them, and every kind of cruelty be practised by your grief, if it will profit you. But if the dead cannot be brought back to life, however much we may beat our breasts, if destiny remains fixed and immoveable forever, not to be changed by any sorrow, however great, and death does not loose his hold of anything that he once has taken away, then let our futile grief be brought to an end. Let us, then, steer our own course, and no longer allow ourselves to be driven to leeward by the force of our misfortune. He is a sorry pilot who lets the waves wring his rudder from his grasp, who leaves the sails to fly loose, and abandons the ship to the storm: but he who boldly grasps the helm and clings to it until the sea closes over him, deserves praise even though he be shipwrecked.

7

———

VII

"But," say you, "sorrow for the loss of one's own children is natural." Who denies it? provided it be reasonable? for we cannot help feeling a pang, and the stoutest-hearted of us are cast down not only at the death of those dearest to us, but even when they leave us on a journey. Nevertheless, the mourning which public opinion enjoins is more than nature insists upon. Observe how intense and yet how brief are the sorrows of dumb animals: we hear a cow lowing for one or two days, nor do mares pursue their wild and senseless gallops for longer: wild beasts after they have tracked their lost cubs throughout the forest, and often visited their plundered dens, quench their rage within a short space of time. Birds circle round their empty nests with loud and piteous cries, yet almost immediately resume their ordinary flight in silence; nor does any creature spend long periods in sorrowing for the loss of its offspring, except man, who encourages his own grief, the measure of which depends not upon his sufferings, but upon his will. You may know that to be utterly broken down by grief is not natural, by observing that the same bereavement inflicts a deeper wound upon women than upon men, upon savages than upon civilized and cultivated persons, upon the unlearned than upon the learned: yet those passions which derive their force from nature are equally powerful in all men: therefore it is clear that a passion of varying strength cannot be a natural one. Fire will burn all people equally, male and female, of every rank and every age: steel will exhibit its cutting power on all bodies alike: and why? Because these things derive their strength from nature, which makes no distinction of persons. Poverty, grief, and ambition,[1] are felt differently by different people, according as they are influenced by habit: a rooted prejudice about the terrors of these things, though they are not really to be feared, makes a man weak and unable to endure them.

8

VIII

Moreover, that which depends upon nature is not weakened by delay, but grief is gradually effaced by time. However obstinate it may be, though it be daily renewed and be exasperated by all attempts to soothe it, yet even this becomes weakened by time, which is the most efficient means of taming its fierceness. You, Marcia, have still a mighty sorrow abiding with you, nevertheless it already appears to have become blunted: it is obstinate and enduring, but not so acute as it was at first: and this also will be taken from you piecemeal by succeeding years. Whenever you are engaged in other pursuits your mind will be relieved from its burden: at present you keep watch over yourself to prevent this. Yet there is a great difference between allowing and forcing yourself to grieve. How much more in accordance with your cultivated taste it would be to put an end to your mourning instead of looking for the end to come, and not to wait for the day when your sorrow shall cease against your will: dismiss it of your own accord.

9

IX

"Why then," you ask, "do we show such persistence in mourning for our friends, if it be not nature that bids us do so?" It is because we never expect that any evil will befall ourselves before it comes, we will not be taught by seeing the misfortunes of others that they are the common inheritance of all men, but imagine that the path which we have begun to tread is free from them and less beset by dangers than that of other people. How many funerals pass our houses? yet we do not think of death. How many untimely deaths? we think only of our son's coming of age, of his service in the army, or of his succession to his father's estate. How many rich men suddenly sink into poverty before our very eyes, without its ever occurring to our minds that our own wealth is exposed to exactly the same risks? When, therefore, misfortune befalls us, we cannot help collapsing all the more completely, because we are struck as it were unawares: a blow which has long been foreseen falls much less heavily upon us. Do you wish to know how completely exposed you are to every stroke of fate, and that the same shafts which have transfixed others are whirling around yourself? Then imagine that you are mounting without sufficient armour to assault some city wall or some strong and lofty position manned by a great host, expect a wound, and suppose that all those stones, arrows, and darts which fill the upper air are aimed at your body: whenever anyone falls at your side or behind your back, exclaim, "Fortune, you will not outwit me, or catch me confident and heedless: I know what you are preparing to do: you have struck down another, but you aimed at me." Whoever looks upon his own affairs as though he were at the point of death? which of us ever dares to think about banishment, want, or mourning? who, if advised to meditate upon these subjects, would not reject the idea like an evil omen, and bid it depart from him and alight on the heads of his enemies, or even on that of his untimely adviser? "I never thought it would happen!" How can you think that anything will not happen, when you know that it may happen to many men, and has happened to many? That is a noble verse, and worthy of a nobler source than the stage:—

> "What one hath suffered may befall us
> all."

That man has lost his children: you may lose yours. That man has been convicted: your innocence is in peril. We are deceived and weakened by this delusion, when we suffer what we never foresaw that we possibly could suffer: but by looking forward to the coming of our sorrows we take the sting out of them when they come.

10

X

My Marcia, all these adventitious circumstances which glitter around us, such as children, office in the State, wealth, large halls, vestibules crowded with clients seeking vainly for admittance, a noble name, a wellborn or beautiful wife, and every other thing which depends entirely upon uncertain and changeful fortune, are but furniture which is not our own, but entrusted to us on loan: none of these things are given to us outright: the stage of our lives is adorned with properties gathered from various sources, and soon to be returned to their several owners: some of them will be taken away on the first day, some on the second, and but few will remain till the end. We have, therefore, no grounds for regarding ourselves with complacency, as though the things which surround us were our own: they are only borrowed: we have the use and enjoyment of them for a time regulated by the lender, who controls his own gift: it is our duty always to be able to lay our hands upon what has been lent us with no fixed date for its return, and to restore it when called upon without a murmur: the most detestable kind of debtor is he who rails at his creditor. Hence all our relatives, both those who by the order of their birth we hope will outlive ourselves, and those who themselves most properly wish to die before us, ought to be loved by us as persons whom we cannot be sure of having with us forever, nor even for long. We ought frequently to remind ourselves that we must love the things of this life as we would what is shortly to leave us, or indeed in the very act of leaving us. Whatever gift Fortune bestows upon a man, let him think while he enjoys it, that it will prove as fickle as the goddess from whom it came. Snatch what pleasure you can from your children, allow your children in their turn to take pleasure in your society, and drain every pleasure to the dregs without any delay. We cannot reckon on tonight, nay, I have allowed too long a delay, we cannot reckon on this hour: we must make haste: the enemy presses on behind us: soon that society of yours will be broken up, that pleasant company will be taken by assault and dispersed. Pillage is the universal law: unhappy creatures, know you not that life is but a flight? If you grieve for the death of your son, the fault lies with the time when he was born, for at his birth he was told that death was his doom: it is the law under which he was born, the fate which has pursued him ever since he left his mother's womb. We have come under the dominion of Fortune, and a harsh and unconquerable dominion it is: at her caprice we must suffer all things whether we deserve them or not. She maltreats our bodies with anger, insult, and cruelty: some she burns, the fire being sometimes applied as a punishment and sometimes as a remedy: some she imprisons, allowing it to be done at one time by our enemies, at another by our countrymen: she tosses others naked on the changeful seas, and after their struggle with the waves will not even cast them out upon the sand or the shore, but will

entomb them in the belly of some huge sea-monster: she
wears away others to a skeleton by diverse kinds of disease,
and keeps them long in suspense between life and death:
she is as capricious in her rewards and punishments as a
fickle, whimsical, and careless mistress is with those of her
slaves.

11

XI

Why need we weep over parts of our life? the whole of it calls for tears: new miseries assail us before we have freed ourselves from the old ones. You, therefore, who allow them to trouble you to an unreasonable extent ought especially to restrain yourselves, and to muster all the powers of the human breast to combat your fears and your pains. Moreover, what forgetfulness of your own position and that of mankind is this? You were born a mortal, and you have given birth to mortals: yourself a weak and fragile body, liable to all diseases, can you have hoped to produce anything strong and lasting from such unstable materials? Your son has died: in other words he has reached that goal towards which those whom you regard as more fortunate than your offspring are still hastening: this is the point towards which move at different rates all the crowds which are squabbling in the law courts, sitting in the theatres, praying in the temples. Those whom you love and those whom you despise will both be made equal in the same ashes. This is the meaning of that command, know thyself, which is written on the shrine of the Pythian oracle.

What is man? a potter's vessel, to be broken by the slightest shake or toss: it requires no great storm to rend you asunder: you fall to pieces wherever you strike. What is man? a weakly and frail body, naked, without any natural protection, dependent on the help of others, exposed to all the scorn of Fortune; even when his muscles are well trained he is the prey and the food of the first wild beast he meets, formed of weak and unstable substances, fair in outward feature, but unable to endure cold, heat, or labour, and yet falling to ruin if kept in sloth and idleness, fearing his very victuals, for he is starved if he has them not, and bursts if he has too much. He cannot be kept safe without anxious care, his breath only stays in the body on sufferance, and has no real hold upon it; he starts at every sudden danger, every loud and unexpected noise that reaches his ears. Ever a cause of anxiety to ourselves, diseased and useless as we are, can we be surprised at the death of a creature which can be killed by a single hiccup? Is it a great undertaking to put an end to us? why, smells, tastes, fatigue and want of sleep, food and drink, and the very necessaries of life, are mortal. Whithersoever he moves he straightaway becomes conscious of his weakness, not being able to bear all climates, falling sick after drinking strange water, breathing an air to which he is not accustomed, or from other causes and reasons of the most trifling kind, frail, sickly, entering upon his life with weeping: yet nevertheless what a disturbance this despicable creature makes! what ideas it conceives, forgetting its lowly condition! It exercises its mind upon matters which are immortal and eternal, and arranges the affairs of its grandchildren and great-grandchildren, while death surprises it in the midst of its far-reaching schemes, and what we call old age is but the round of a very few years.

12

XII

Supposing that your sorrow has any method at all, is it your own sufferings or those of him who is gone that it has in view? Why do you grieve over your lost son? is it because you have received no pleasure from him, or because you would have received more had he lived longer? If you answer that you have received no pleasure from him you make your loss more endurable: for men miss less when lost what has given them no enjoyment or gladness. If, again, you admit that you have received much pleasure, it is your duty not to complain of that part which you have lost, but to return thanks for that which you have enjoyed. His rearing alone ought to have brought you a sufficient return for your labours, for it can hardly be that those who take the greatest pains to rear puppies, birds, and suchlike paltry objects of amusement derive a certain pleasure from the sight and touch and fawning caresses of these dumb creatures, and yet that those who rear children should not find their reward in doing so. Thus, even though his industry may have gained nothing for you, his carefulness may have saved nothing for you, his foresight may have given you no advice, yet you found sufficient reward in having owned him and loved him. "But," say you, "it might have lasted longer." True, but you have been better dealt with than if you had never had a son, for, supposing you were given your choice, which is the better lot, to be happy for a short time or not at all? It is better to enjoy pleasures which soon leave us than to enjoy none at all. Which, again, would you choose? to have had one who was a disgrace to you, and who merely filled the position and owned the name of your son, or one of such noble character as your son's was? a youth who soon grew discreet and dutiful, soon became a husband and a father, soon became eager for public honours, and soon obtained the priesthood, winning his way to all these admirable things with equally admirable speed. It falls to scarcely anyone's lot to enjoy great prosperity, and also to enjoy it for a long time: only a dull kind of happiness can last for long and accompany us to the end of our lives. The immortal gods, who did not intend to give you a son for long, gave you one who was straightaway what another would have required long training to become. You cannot even say that you have been specially marked by the gods for misfortune because you have had no pleasure in your son. Look at any company of people, whether they be known to you or not: everywhere you will see some who have endured greater misfortunes than your own. Great generals and princes have undergone like bereavements: mythology tells us that the gods themselves are not exempt from them, its aim, I suppose, being to lighten our sorrow at death by the thought that even deities are subject to it. Look around, I repeat, at everyone: you cannot mention any house so miserable as not to find comfort in the fact of another being yet more miserable. I do not, by Hercules, think so ill of your principles as to suppose that you would bear your sorrow more lightly were I to show you an enormous company of mourners: that is a spiteful sort of consolation which we derive from the number of our fellow-sufferers: nevertheless I will quote some instances, not indeed in order to teach you that this often befalls men, for it is absurd to multiply examples of man's mortality, but to let you know that there have been many who have lightened their misfortunes by patient endurance of them. I will begin with the luckiest man of all. Lucius Sulla lost his son, yet this did not impair either the spitefulness or the brilliant valour which he displayed at the expense of his enemies and his countrymen alike, nor did it make him appear to have assumed his well-known title untruly that he did so after his son's death, fearing neither the hatred of men, by whose sufferings that excessive prosperity of his was purchased, nor the ill-will of the gods, to whom it was a reproach that Sulla should be so truly The Fortunate. What, however, Sulla's real character was may pass among questions still undecided: even his enemies will admit that he took up arms with honour, and laid them aside with honour: his example proves the point at issue, that an evil which befalls even the most prosperous cannot be one of the first magnitude.

13

XIII

That Greece cannot boast unduly of that father who, being in the act of offering sacrifice when he heard the news of his son's death, merely ordered the flute-player to be silent, and removed the garland from his head, but accomplished all the rest of the ceremony in due form, is due to a Roman, Pulvillus the high priest. When he was in the act of holding the doorpost[1] and dedicating the Capitol the news of his son's death was brought to him. He pretended not to hear it, and pronounced the form of words proper for the high priest on such an occasion, without his prayer being interrupted by a single groan, begging that Jupiter would show himself gracious, at the very instant that he heard his son's name mentioned as dead. Do you imagine that this man's mourning knew no end, if the first day and the first shock could not drive him, though a father, away from the public altar of the State, or cause him to mar the ceremony of dedication by words of ill omen? Worthy, indeed, of the most exalted priesthood was he who ceased not to revere the gods even when they were angry. Yet he, after he had gone home, filled his eyes with tears, said a few words of lamentation, and performed the rites with which it was then customary to honour the dead, resumed the expression of countenance which he had worn in the Capitol.

Paulus,[2] about the time of his magnificent triumph, in which he drove Perses in chains before his car, gave two of his sons to be adopted into other families, and buried those whom he had kept for himself. What, think you, must those whom he kept have been, when Scipio was one of those whom he gave away? It was not without emotion that the Roman people looked upon Paulus's empty chariot:[3] nevertheless he made a speech to them, and returned thanks to the gods for having granted his prayer: for he had prayed that, if any offering to Nemesis were due in consequence of the stupendous victory which he had won, it might be paid at his own expense rather than at that of his country. Do you see how magnanimously he bore his loss? he even congratulated himself on being left childless, though who had more to suffer by such a change? he lost at once his comforters and his helpers. Yet Perses did not have the pleasure of seeing Paulus look sorrowful.

14

XIV

Why should I lead you on through the endless series of great men and pick out the unhappy ones, as though it were not more difficult to find happy ones? For how few households have remained possessed of all their members until the end? what one is there that has not suffered some loss? Take any one year you please and name the consuls for it: if you like, that of [1]Lucius Bibulus and Gaius Caesar; you will see that, though these colleagues were each other's bitterest enemies, yet their fortunes agreed. Lucius Bibulus, a man more remarkable for goodness than for strength of character, had both his sons murdered at the same time, and even insulted by the Egyptian soldiery, so that the agent of his bereavement was as much a subject for tears as the bereavement itself. Nevertheless Bibulus, who during the whole of his year of office had remained hidden in his house, to cast reproach upon his colleague Caesar on the day following that upon which he heard of both his sons' deaths, came forth and went through the routine business of his magistracy. Who could devote less than one day to mourning for two sons?

Thus soon did he end his mourning for his children, although he had mourned a whole year for his consulship. Gaius Caesar, after having traversed Britain, and not allowed even the ocean to set bounds to his successes, heard of the death of his daughter, which hurried on the crisis of affairs. Already Gnaeus Pompeius stood before his eyes, a man who would ill endure that anyone besides himself should become a great power in the State, and one who was likely to place a check upon his advancement, which he had regarded as onerous even when each gained by the other's rise: yet within three days' time he resumed his duties as general, and conquered his grief as quickly as he was wont to conquer everything else.

XV

Why need I remind you of the deaths of the other Caesars, whom Fortune appears to me sometimes to have outraged in order that even by their deaths they might be useful to mankind, by proving that not even they, although they were styled "sons of gods," and "fathers of gods to come," could exercise the same power over their own fortunes which they did over those of others? The Emperor Augustus lost his children and his grandchildren, and after all the family of Caesar had perished was obliged to prop his empty house by adopting a son: yet he bore his losses as bravely as though he were already personally concerned in the honour of the gods, and as though it were especially to his interest that no one should complain of the injustice of Heaven. Tiberius Caesar lost both the son whom he begot and the son whom he adopted, yet he himself pronounced a panegyric upon his son from the Rostra, and stood in full view of the corpse, which merely had a curtain on one side to prevent the eyes of the high priest resting upon the dead body, and did not change his countenance, though all the Romans wept: he gave Sejanus, who stood by his side, a proof of how patiently he could endure the loss of his relatives. See you not what numbers of most eminent men there have been, none of whom have been spared by this blight which prostrates us all: men, too, adorned with every grace of character, and every distinction that public or private life can confer. It appears as though this plague moved in a regular orbit, and spread ruin and desolation among us all without distinction of persons, all being alike its prey. Bid any number of individuals tell you the story of their lives: you will find that all have paid some penalty for being born.

XVI

I know what you will say: "You quote men as examples: you forget that it is a woman that you are trying to console." Yet who would say that nature has dealt grudgingly with the minds of women, and stunted their virtues? Believe me, they have the same intellectual power as men, and the same capacity for honourable and generous action. If trained to do so, they are just as able to endure sorrow or labour. Ye good gods, do I say this in that very city in which Lucretia and Brutus removed the yoke of kings from the necks of the Romans? We owe liberty to Brutus, but we owe Brutus to Lucretia—in which Cloelia, for the sublime courage with which she scorned both the enemy and the river, has been almost reckoned as a man. The statue of Cloelia, mounted on horseback, in that busiest of thoroughfares, the Sacred Way, continually reproaches the youth of the present day, who never mount anything but a cushioned seat in a carriage, with journeying in such a fashion through that very city in which we have enrolled even women among our knights. If you wish me to point out to you examples of women who have bravely endured the loss of their children, I shall not go far afield to search for them: in one family I can quote two Cornelias, one the daughter of Scipio, and the mother of the Gracchi, who made acknowledgment of the birth of her twelve children by burying them all: nor was it so hard to do this in the case of the others, whose birth and death were alike unknown to the public, but she beheld the murdered and unburied corpses of both Tiberius Gracchus and Gaius Gracchus, whom even those who will not call them good must admit were great men. Yet to those who tried to console her and called her unfortunate, she answered, "I shall never cease to call myself happy, because I am the mother of the Gracchi." Cornelia, the wife of Livius Drusus, lost by the hands of an unknown assassin a young son of great distinction, who was treading in the footsteps of the Gracchi, and was murdered in his own house just when he had so many bills half way through the process of becoming law: nevertheless she bore the untimely and unavenged death of her son with as lofty a spirit as he had shown in carrying his laws. Will you not, Marcia, forgive Fortune because she has not refrained from striking you with the darts with which she launched at the Scipios, and the mothers and daughters of the Scipios, and with which she has attacked the Caesars themselves? Life is full of misfortunes; our path is beset with them: no one can make a long peace, nay, scarcely an armistice with Fortune. You, Marcia, have borne four children: now they say that no dart which is hurled into a close column of soldiers can fail to hit one—ought you then to wonder at not having been able to lead along such a company without exciting the ill-will of Fortune, or suffering loss at her hands? "But," say you, "Fortune has treated me unfairly, for she not only has bereaved me of my son, but chose my best beloved to deprive me of." Yet you never can say that you have been wronged, if you divide the stakes equally with an antagonist who is stronger than yourself: Fortune has left you two daughters, and their children: she has not even taken away altogether him who you now mourn for, forgetful of his elder brother: you have two daughters by him, who if you support them ill will prove great burdens, but if well, great comforts to you. You ought to prevail upon yourself, when you see them, to let them remind you of your son, and not of your grief. When a husbandman's trees have either been torn up, roots and all, by the wind, or broken off short by the force of a hurricane, he takes care of what is left of their stock, straightaway plants seeds or cuttings in the place of those which he has lost, and in a moment—for time is as swift in repairing losses as in causing them—more nourishing trees are growing than were there before. Take, then, in the place of your Metilius these his two daughters, and by their twofold consolation lighten your single sorrow. True, human nature is so constituted as to love nothing so much as what it has lost, and our yearning after those who have been taken from us makes us judge unfairly of those who are left to us: nevertheless, if you choose to reckon up how merciful Fortune has been to you even in her anger, you will feel that you have more than enough to console you. Look at all your grandchildren, and your two daughters: and say also, Marcia:—"I should indeed be cast down, if everyone's fortune followed his deserts, and if no evil ever befell good men: but as it is I perceive that no distinction is made, and that the bad and the good are both harassed alike."

17

XVII

"Still, it is a sad thing to lose a young man whom you have brought up, just as he was becoming a defence and a pride both to his mother and to his country." No one denies that it is sad: but it is the common lot of mortals. You were born to lose others, to be lost, to hope, to fear, to destroy your own peace and that of others, to fear and yet to long for death, and, worst of all, never to know what your real position is. If you were about to journey to Syracuse, and someone were to say:—"Learn beforehand all the discomforts, and all the pleasures of your coming voyage, and then set sail. The sights which you will enjoy will be as follows: first, you will see the island itself, now separated from Italy by a narrow strait, but which, we know, once formed part of the mainland. The sea suddenly broke through, and

> 'Sever'd Sicilia from the western
> shore.'[1]

Next, as you will be able to sail close to Charybdis, of

which the poets have sung, you will see that greediest of whirlpools, quite smooth if no south wind be blowing, but whenever there is a gale from that quarter, sucking down ships into a huge and deep abyss. You will see the fountain of Arethusa, so famed in song, with its waters bright and pellucid to the very bottom, and pouring forth an icy stream which it either finds on the spot or else plunges it under ground, conveys it thither as a separate river beneath so many seas, free from any mixture of less pure water, and there brings it again to the surface. You will see a harbour which is more sheltered than all the others in the world, whether they be natural or improved by human art for the protection of shipping; so safe, that even the most violent storms are powerless to disturb it. You will see the place where the power of Athens was broken, where that natural prison, hewn deep among precipices of rock, received so many thousands of captives: you will see the great city itself, occupying a wider site than many capitals, an extremely warm resort in winter, where not a single day passes without sunshine: but when you have observed all this, you must remember that the advantages of its winter climate are counterbalanced by a hot and pestilential summer: that here will be the tyrant Dionysius, the destroyer of freedom, of justice, and of law, who is greedy of power even after conversing with Plato, and of life even after he has been exiled; that he will burn some, flog others, and behead others for slight offences; that he will exercise his lust upon both sexes... You have now heard all that can attract you thither, all that can deter you from going: now, then, either set sail or remain at home!" If, after this declaration, anybody were to say that he wished to go to Syracuse, he could blame no one but himself for what befell him there, because he would not stumble upon it unknowingly, but would have gone thither fully aware of what was before him. To everyone Nature says: "I do not deceive any person. If you choose to have children, they may be handsome, or they may be deformed; perhaps they will be born dumb. One of them may perhaps prove the saviour of his country, or perhaps its betrayer. You need not despair of their being raised to such honour that for their sake no one will dare to speak evil of you: yet remember that they may reach such a pitch of infamy as themselves to become curses to you. There is nothing to prevent their performing the last offices for you, and your panegyric being spoken by your children: but hold yourself prepared nevertheless to place a son as boy, man, or greybeard, upon the funeral pyre: for years have nothing to do with the matter, since every sort of funeral in which a parent buries his child must alike be untimely.[2]If you still choose to rear children, after I have explained these conditions to you, you render yourself incapable of blaming the gods, for they never guaranteed anything to you."

18

XVIII

You may make this simile apply to your whole entrance into life. I have explained to you what attractions and what drawbacks there would be if you were thinking of going to Syracuse: now suppose that I were to come and give you advice when you were going to be born. "You are about," I should say, "to enter a city of which both gods and men are citizens, a city which contains the whole universe, which is bound by irrevocable and eternal laws, and wherein the heavenly bodies run their unwearied courses: you will see therein innumerable twinkling stars, and the sun, whose single light pervades every place, who by his daily course marks the times of day and night, and by his yearly course makes a more equal division between summer and winter. You will see his place taken by night by the moon, who borrows at her meetings with her brother a gentle and softer light, and who at one time is invisible, at another hangs full faced above the Earth, ever waxing and waning, each phase unlike the last. You will see five stars, moving in the opposite direction to the others, stemming the whirl of the skies towards the West: on the slightest motions of these depend the fortunes of nations, and according as the aspect of the planets is auspicious or malignant, the greatest empires rise and fall: you will see with wonder the gathering clouds, the falling showers, the zigzag lightning, the crashing together of the heavens. When, sated with the wonders above, you turn your eyes towards the Earth, they will be met by objects of a different yet equally admirable aspect: on one side a boundless expanse of open plains, on another the towering peaks of lofty and snow-clad mountains: the downward course of rivers, some streams running eastward, some westward from the same source: the woods which wave even on the mountain tops, the vast forests with all the creatures that dwell therein, and the confused harmony of the birds: the variously-placed cities, the nations which natural obstacles keep secluded from the world, some of whom withdraw themselves to lofty mountains, while others dwell in fear and trembling on the sloping banks of rivers: the crops which are assisted by cultivation, and the trees which bear fruit even without it: the rivers that flow gently through the meadows, the lovely bays and shores that curve inwards to form harbours: the countless islands scattered over the main, which break and spangle the seas. What of the brilliancy of stones and gems, the gold that rolls amid the sands of rushing streams, the heaven-born fires that burst forth from the midst of the earth and even from the midst of the sea; the ocean itself, that binds land to land, dividing the nations by its threefold indentations, and boiling up with mighty rage? Swimming upon its waves, making them disturbed and swelling without wind, you will see animals exceeding the size of any that belong to the land, some clumsy and requiring others to guide their movements, some swift and moving faster than the utmost efforts of rowers, some of them that drink in the waters and blow them out again to the great perils of those who sail near them: you will see here ships seeking for unknown lands: you will see that man's audacity leaves nothing unattempted, and you will yourself be both a witness and a sharer in great attempts. You will both learn and teach the arts by which men's lives are supplied with necessaries, are adorned, and are ruled: but in this same place there will be a thousand pestilences fatal to both body and mind, there will be wars and highway robberies, poisonings and shipwrecks, extremes of climate and excesses of body, untimely griefs for our dearest ones, and death for ourselves, of which we cannot tell whether it will be easy or by torture at the hands of the executioner." Now consider and weigh carefully in your own mind which you would choose. If you wish to enjoy these blessings you must pass through these pains. Do you answer that you choose to live? "Of course." Nay, I thought you would not enter upon that of which the least diminution causes pain. Live, then, as has been agreed on. You say, "No one has asked my opinion." Our parents' opinion was taken about us, when, knowing what the conditions of life are, they brought us into it.

19

___

XIX

But, to come to topics of consolation, in the first place consider if you please to what our remedies must be applied, and next, in what way. It is regret for the absence of his loved one which causes a mourner to grieve: yet it is clear that this in itself is bearable enough; for we do not weep at their being absent or intending to be absent during their lifetime, although when they leave our sight we have no more pleasure in them. What tortures us, therefore, is an idea. Now every evil is just as great as we consider it to be: we have, therefore, the remedy in our own hands. Let us suppose that they are on a journey, and let us deceive ourselves: we have sent them away, or, rather, we have sent them on in advance to a place whither we shall soon follow them.[1] Besides this, mourners are wont to suffer from the thought, "I shall have no one to protect me, no one to avenge me when I am scorned." To use a very disreputable but very true mode of consolation, I may say that in our country the loss of children bestows more influence than it takes away, and loneliness, which used to bring the aged to ruin, now makes them so powerful that some old men have pretended to pick quarrels with their sons, have disowned their own children, and have made themselves childless by their own act. I know what you will say: "My own losses do not grieve me:" and indeed a man does not deserve to be consoled if he is sorry for his son's death as he would be for that of a slave, who is capable of seeing anything in his son beyond his son's self. What then, Marcia, is it that grieves you? is it that your son has died, or that he did not live long? If it be his having died, then you ought always to have grieved, for you always knew that he would die. Reflect that the dead suffer no evils, that all those stories which make us dread the nether world are mere fables, that he who dies need fear no darkness, no prison, no blazing streams of fire, no river of Lethe, no judgment seat before which he must appear, and that Death is such utter freedom that he need fear no more despots. All that is a fantasy of the poets, who have terrified us without a cause. Death is a release from and an end of all pains: beyond it our sufferings cannot extend: it restores us to the peaceful rest in which we lay before we were born. If anyone pities the dead, he ought also to pity those who have not been born. Death is neither a good nor a bad thing, for that alone which is something can be a good or a bad thing: but that which is nothing, and reduces all things to nothing, does not hand us over to either fortune, because good and bad require some material to work upon. Fortune cannot take hold of that which Nature has let go, nor can a man be unhappy if he is nothing. Your son has passed beyond the border of the country where men are forced to labour; he has reached deep and everlasting peace. He feels no fear of want, no anxiety about his riches, no stings of lust that tears the heart in guise of pleasure: he knows no envy of another's prosperity, he is not crushed by the weight of his own; even his chaste ears are not wounded by any ribaldry: he is menaced by no disaster, either to his country or to himself. He does not hang, full of anxiety, upon the issue of events, to reap even greater uncertainty as his reward: he has at last taken up a position from which nothing can dislodge him, where nothing can make him afraid.

20

XX

O how little do men understand their own misery, that they do not praise and look forward to death as the best discovery of Nature, whether because it hedges in happiness, or because it drives away misery: because it puts an end to the sated weariness of old age, cuts down youth in its bloom while still full of hope of better things, or calls home childhood before the harsher stages of life are reached: it is the end of all men, a relief to many, a desire to some, and it treats none so well as those to whom it comes before they call for it. Death frees the slave though his master wills it not, it lightens the captive's chains: it leads out of prison those whom headstrong power has forbidden to quit it: it points out to exiles, whose minds and eyes are ever turned towards their own country, that it makes no difference under what people's soil one lies. When Fortune has unjustly divided the common stock, and has given over one man to another, though they were born with equal rights, Death makes them all equal. After Death no one acts any more at another's bidding: in death no man suffers any more from the sense of his low position. It is open to all: it was what your father, Marcia, longed for: it is this, I say, that renders it no misery to be born, which enables me to face the threatenings of misfortune without quailing, and to keep my mind unharmed and able to command itself. I have a last appeal. I see before me crosses not all alike, but differently made by different peoples: some hang a man head downwards, some force a stick upwards through his groin, some stretch out his arms on a forked gibbet. I see cords, scourges, and instruments of torture for each limb and each joint: but I see Death also. There are bloodthirsty enemies, there are overbearing fellow-country-men, but where they are there I see Death also. Slavery is not grievous if a man can gain his freedom by one step as soon as he becomes tired of thralldom. Life, it is thanks to Death that I hold thee so dear. Think how great a blessing is a timely death, how many have been injured by living longer than they ought. If sickness had carried off that glory and support of the empire Gnaeus Pompeius, at Naples, he would have died the undoubted head of the Roman people, but as it was, a short extension of time cast him down from his pinnacle of fame: he beheld his legions slaughtered before his eyes: and what a sad relic of that battle, in which the Senate formed the first line, was the survival of the general. He saw his Egyptian butcher, and offered his body, hallowed by so many victories, to a guardsman's sword, although even had he been unhurt, he would have regretted his safety: for what could have been more infamous than that a Pompeius should owe his life to the clemency of a king? If Marcus Cicero had fallen at the time when he avoided those daggers which Catiline aimed equally at him and at his country, he might have died as the saviour of the commonwealth which he had set free: if his death had even followed upon that of his daughter, he might have died happy. He would not then have seen swords drawn for the slaughter of Roman citizens, the goods of the murdered divided among the murderers, that men might pay from their own purse the price of their own blood, the public auction of the consul's spoil in the civil war, the public letting out of murder to be done, brigandage, war, pillage, hosts of Catilines. Would it not have been a good thing for Marcus Cato if the sea had swallowed him up when he was returning from Cyprus after sequestrating the king's hereditary possessions, even if that very money which he was bringing to pay the soldiers in the civil war had been lost with him? He certainly would have been able to boast that no one would dare to do wrong in the presence of Cato: as it was, the extension of his life for a very few more years forced one who was born for personal and political freedom to flee from Caesar and to become Pompeius's follower. Premature death therefore did him no evil: indeed, it put an end to the power of any evil to hurt him.

XXI

"Yet," say you, "he perished too soon and untimely." In the first place, suppose that he had lived to extreme old age: let him continue alive to the extreme limits of human existence: how much is it after all? Born for a very brief space of time, we regard this life as an inn which we are soon to quit that it may be made ready for the coming guest. Do I speak of our lives, which we know roll away incredibly fast? Reckon up the centuries of cities: you will find that even those which boast of their antiquity have not existed for long. All human works are brief and fleeting; they take up no part whatever of infinite time. Tried by the standard of the universe, we regard this Earth of ours, with all its cities, nations, rivers, and seaboard as a mere point: our life occupies less than a point when compared with all time, the measure of which exceeds that of the world, for indeed the world is contained many times in it. Of what importance, then, can it be to lengthen that which, however much you add to it, will never be much more than nothing? We can only make our lives long by one expedient, that is, by being satisfied with their length: you may tell me of long-lived men, whose length of days has been celebrated by tradition, you may assign a hundred and ten years apiece to them: yet when you allow your mind to conceive the idea of eternity, there will be no difference between the shortest and the longest life, if you compare the time during which anyone has been alive with that during which he has not been alive. In the next place, when he died his life was complete: he had lived as long as he needed to live: there was nothing left for him to accomplish. All men do not grow old at the same age, nor indeed do all animals: some are wearied out by life at fourteen years of age, and what is only the first stage of life with man is their extreme limit of longevity. To each man a varying length of days has been assigned: no one dies before his time, because he was not destined to live any longer than he did. Everyone's end is fixed, and will always remain where it has been placed: neither industry nor favour will move it on any further. Believe, then, that you lost him by advice: he took all that was his own,

> "And reached the goal allotted to his
>   life,"

so you need not burden yourself with the thought, "He might have lived longer." His life has not been cut short, nor does chance ever cut short our years: every man receives as much as was promised to him: the Fates go their own way, and neither add anything nor take away anything from what they have once promised. Prayers and endeavours are all in vain: each man will have as much life as his first day placed to his credit: from the time when he first saw the light he has entered on the path that leads to death, and is drawing nearer to his doom: those same years which were added to his youth were subtracted from his life. We all fall into this mistake of supposing that it is only old men, already in the decline of life, who are drawing near to death, whereas our first infancy, our youth, indeed every time of life leads thither. The Fates ply their own work: they take from us the consciousness of our death, and, the better to conceal its approaches, death lurks under the very names we give to life: infancy changes into boyhood, maturity swallows up the boy, old age the man: these stages themselves, if you reckon them properly, are so many losses.

22

XXII

Do you complain, Marcia, that your son did not live as long as he might have done? How do you know that it was to his advantage to live longer? whether his interest was not served by this death? Whom can you find at the present time whose fortunes are grounded on such sure foundations that they have nothing to fear in the future? All human affairs are evanescent and perishable, nor is any part of our life so frail and liable to accident as that which we especially enjoy. We ought, therefore, to pray for death when our fortune is at its best, because so great is the uncertainty and turmoil in which we live, that we can be sure of nothing but what is past. Think of your son's handsome person, which you had guarded in perfect purity among all the temptations of a voluptuous capital. Who could have undertaken to keep that clear of all diseases, so that it might preserve its beauty of form unimpaired even to old age? Think of the many taints of the mind: for fine dispositions do not always continue to their life's end to make good the promise of their youth, but have often broken down: either extravagance, all the more shameful for being indulged in late in life, takes possession of men and makes their well-begun lives end in disgrace, or they devote their entire thoughts to the eating-house and the belly, and they become interested in nothing save what they shall eat and what they shall drink. Add to this conflagrations, falling houses, shipwrecks, the agonizing operations of surgeons, who cut pieces of bone out of men's living bodies, plunge their whole hands into their entrails, and inflict more than one kind of pain to effect the cure of shameful diseases. After these comes exile; your son was not more innocent than Rutilius: imprisonment; he was not wiser than Socrates: the piercing of one's breast by a self-inflicted wound; he was not of holier life than Cato. When you look at these examples, you will perceive that nature deals very kindly with those whom she puts speedily in a place of safety because there awaited them the payment of some such price as this for their lives. Nothing is so deceptive, nothing is so treacherous as human life; by Hercules, were it not given to men before they could form an opinion, no one would take it. Not to be born, therefore, is the happiest lot of all, and the nearest thing to this, I imagine, is that we should soon finish our strife here and be restored again to our former rest. Recall to your mind that time, so painful to you, during which Sejanus handed over your father as a present to his client Satrius Secundus: he was angry with him about something or other which he had said with too great freedom, because he was not able to keep silence and see Sejanus climbing up to take his seat upon our necks, which would have been bad enough had he been placed there by his master. He was decreed the honour of a statue, to be set up in the theatre of Pompeius, which had been burned down and was being restored by Caesar. Cordus exclaimed that "Now the theatre was really destroyed." What then? should he not burst with spite at a Sejanus being set up over the ashes of Gnaeus Pompeius, at a faithless soldier being commemorated within the memorial of a consummate commander?

The inscription was put up:[1] and those keen-scented hounds whom Sejanus used to feed on human blood, to make them tame towards himself and fierce to all the world beside, began to bay around their victim and even to make premature snaps at him. What was he to do? If he chose to live, he must gain the consent of Sejanus; if to die, he must gain that of his daughter; and neither of them could have been persuaded to grant it: he therefore determined to deceive his daughter, and having taken a bath in order to weaken himself still further, he retired to his bedchamber on the pretence of taking a meal there. After dismissing his slaves he threw some of the food out of the window, that he might appear to have eaten it: then he took no supper, making the excuse that he had already had enough food in his chamber. This he continued to do on the second and the third day: the fourth betrayed his condition by his bodily weakness; so, embracing you, "My dearest daughter," said he, "from whom I have never throughout your whole life concealed aught but this, I have begun my journey towards death, and have already travelled halfway thither. You cannot and you ought not to call me back." So saying he ordered all light to be excluded from the room and shut himself up in the darkness. When his determination became known there was a general feeling of pleasure at the prey being snatched out of the jaws of those ravening wolves. His prosecutors, at the instance of Sejanus, went to the judgment-seat of the consuls, complained that Cordus was dying, and begged the consuls to interpose to prevent his doing what they themselves had driven him to do; so true was it that Cordus appeared to them to be escaping: an important matter was at stake, namely, whether the accused should lose the right to die. While this point was being debated, and the prosecutors were going to attend the court a second time, he had set himself free from them. Do you see, Marcia, how suddenly evil days come upon a man? and do you weep because one of your family could not avoid dying? one of your family was within a very little of not being allowed to die.

XXIII

Besides the fact that everything that is future is uncertain, and the only certainty is that it is more likely to turn out ill than well, our spirits find the path to the Gods above easiest when it is soon allowed to leave the society of mankind, because it has then contracted fewest impurities to weigh it down: if set free before they become hardened worldlings, before earthly things have sunk too deep into them, they fly all the more lightly back to the place from whence they came, and all the more easily wash away the stains and defilements which they may have contracted. Great minds never love to linger long in the body: they are eager to burst its bonds and escape from it, they chafe at the narrowness of their prison, having been wont to wander through space, and from aloft in the upper air to look down with contempt upon human affairs. Hence it is that Plato declares that the wise man's mind is entirely given up to death, longs for it, contemplates it, and through his eagerness for it is always striving after things which lie beyond this life. Why, Marcia, when you saw him while yet young displaying the wisdom of age, with a mind that could rise superior to all sensual enjoyments, faultless and without a blemish, able to win riches without greediness, public office without ambition, pleasure without extravagance, did you suppose it would long be your lot to keep him safe by your side? Whatever has arrived at perfection, is ripe for dissolution. Consummate virtue flees away and betakes itself out of our sight, and those things which come to maturity in the first stage of their being do not wait for the last. The brighter a fire glows, the sooner it goes out: it lasts longer when it is made up with bad and slowly burning fuel, and shows a dull light through a cloud of smoke: its being poorly fed makes it linger all the longer. So also the more brilliant men's minds, the shorter lived they are: for when there is no room for further growth, the end is near. Fabianus tells us, what our parents themselves have seen, that there was at Rome a boy of gigantic stature, exceeding that of a man: but he soon died, and every sensible person always said that he would soon die, for he could not live to reach the age which he had assumed before it was due. So it is: too complete maturity is a proof that destruction is near and the end approaches when growth is over.

XXIV

egin to reckon his age, not by years, but by virtues: he lived long enough. He was left as a ward in the care of guardians up to his fourteenth year, and never passed out of that of his mother: when he had a household of his own he was loath to leave yours, and continued to dwell under his mother's roof, though few sons can endure to live under their father's. Though a youth whose height, beauty, and vigour of body destined him for the army, yet he refused to serve, that he might not be separated from you. Consider, Marcia, how seldom mothers who live in separate houses see their children: consider how they lose and pass in anxiety all those years during which they have sons in the army, and you will see that this time, none of which you lost, was of considerable extent: he never went out of your sight: it was under your eyes that he applied himself to the cultivation of an admirable intellect and one which would have rivaled that of his grandfather, had it not been hindered by shyness, which has concealed many men's accomplishments: though a youth of unusual beauty, and living among such throngs of women who made it their business to seduce men, he gratified the wishes of none of them, and when the effrontery of some led them so far as actually to tempt him, he blushed as deeply at having found favour in their eyes as though he had been guilty. By this holiness of life he caused himself, while yet quite a boy, to be thought worthy of the priesthood, which no doubt he owed to his mother's influence; but even his mother's influence would have had no weight if the candidate for whom it was exerted had been unfit for the post. Dwell upon these virtues, and nurse your son as it were in your lap: now he is more at leisure to respond to your caresses, he has nothing to call him away from you, he will never be an anxiety or a sorrow to you. You have grieved at the only grief so good a son could cause you: all else is beyond the power of fortune to harm, and is full of pleasure, if only you know how to make use of your son, if you do but know what his most precious quality was. It is merely the outward semblance of your son that has perished, his likeness, and that not a very good one; he himself is immortal, and is now in a far better state, set free from the burden of all that was not his own, and left simply by himself: all this apparatus which you see about us of bones and sinews, this covering of skin, this face, these our servants the hands, and all the rest of our environment, are but chains and darkness to the soul: they overwhelm it, choke it, corrupt it, fill it with false ideas, and keep it at a distance from its own true sphere: it has to struggle continually against this burden of the flesh, lest it be dragged down and sunk by it. It ever strives to rise up again to the place from whence it was sent down on Earth: there eternal rest awaits it, there it will behold what is pure and clear, in place of what is foul and turbid.

XXV

You need not, therefore, hasten to the burial-place of your son: that which lies there is but the worst part of him and that which gave him most trouble, only bones and ashes, which are no more parts of him than clothes or other coverings of his body. He is complete, and without leaving any part of himself behind on Earth has taken wing and gone away altogether: he has tarried a brief space above us while his soul was being cleansed and purified from the vices and rust which all mortal lives must contract, and from thence he will rise to the high heavens and join the souls of the blessed: a saintly company will welcome him thither—Scipios and Catos; and among the rest of those who have held life cheap and set themselves free, thanks to death, albeit all there are alike akin, your father, Marcia, will embrace his grandson as he rejoices in the unwonted light, will teach him the motion of the stars which are so near to them, and introduce him with joy into all the secrets of nature, not by guesswork but by real knowledge. Even as a stranger is grateful to one who shows him the way about an unknown city, so is a searcher after the causes of what he sees in the heavens to one of his own family who can explain them to him. He will delight in gazing deep down upon the Earth, for it is a delight to look from aloft at what one has left below. Bear yourself, therefore, Marcia, as though you were placed before the eyes of your father and your son, yet not such as you knew them, but far loftier beings, placed in a higher sphere. Blush, then, to do any mean or common action, or to weep for those your relatives who have been changed for the better. Free to roam through the open, boundless realms of the ever-living universe, they are not hindered in their course by intervening seas, lofty mountains, impassable valleys, or the treacherous flats of the Syrtes: they find a level path everywhere, are swift and ready of motion, and are permeated in their turn by the stars and dwell together with them.

XXVI

Imagine then, Marcia, that your father, whose influence over you was as great as yours over your son, no longer in that frame of mind in which he deplored the civil wars, or in which he forever proscribed those who would have proscribed him, but in a mood as much more joyful as his abode now is higher than of old, is saying, as he looks down from the height of heaven, "My daughter, why does this sorrow possess you for so long? why do you live in such ignorance of the truth, as to think that your son has been unfairly dealt with because he has returned to his ancestors in his prime, without decay of body or mind, leaving his family flourishing? Do you not know with what storms Fortune unsettles everything? how she proves kind and compliant to none save to those who have the fewest possible dealings with her? Need I remind you of kings who would have been the happiest of mortals had death sooner withdrawn them from the ruin which was approaching them? or of Roman generals, whose greatness, had but a few years been taken from their lives, would have wanted nothing to render it complete? or of men of the highest distinction and noblest birth who have calmly offered their necks to the stroke of a soldier's sword? Look at your father and your grandfather: the former fell into the hands of a foreign murderer: I allowed no man to take any liberties with me, and by abstinence from food showed that my spirit was as great as my writings had represented it. Why, then, should that member of our household who died most happily of all be mourned in it the longest? We have all assembled together, and, not being plunged in utter darkness, we see that with you on Earth there is nothing to be wished for, nothing grand or magnificent, but all is mean, sad, anxious, and hardly receives a fractional part of the clear light in which we dwell. I need not say that here are no frantic charges of rival armies, no fleets shattering one another, no parricides, actual or meditated, no courts where men babble over lawsuits for days together, here is nothing underhand, all hearts and minds are open and unveiled, our life is public and known to all, and that we command a view of all time and of things to come. I used to take pleasure in compiling the history of what took place in one century among a few people in the most out-of-the-way corner of the world: here I enjoy the spectacle of all the centuries, the whole chain of events from age to age as long as years have been. I may view kingdoms when they rise and when they fall, and behold the ruin of cities and the new channels made by the sea. If it will be any consolation to you in your bereavement to know that it is the common lot of all, be assured that nothing will continue to stand in the place in which it now stands, but that time will lay everything low and bear it away with itself: it will sport, not only with men—for how small a part are they of the dominion of Fortune?—but with districts, provinces, quarters of the world: it will efface entire mountains, and in other places will pile new rocks on high: it will dry up seas, change the course of rivers, destroy the intercourse of nation with nation, and break up the communion and fellowship of the human race: in other regions it will swallow up cities by opening vast chasms in the earth, will shake them with earthquakes, will breathe forth pestilence from the nether world, cover all habitable ground with inundations and destroy every creature in the flooded world, or burn up all mortals by a huge conflagration. When the time shall arrive for the world to be brought to an end, that it may begin its life anew, all the forces of nature will perish in conflict with one another, the stars will be dashed together, and all the lights which now gleam in regular order in various parts of the sky will then blaze in one fire with all their fuel burning at once. Then we also, the souls of the blest and the heirs of eternal life, whenever God thinks fit to reconstruct the universe, when all things are settling down again, we also, being a small accessory to the universal wreck,[1] shall be changed into our old elements. Happy is your son, Marcia, in that he already knows this."

NOTES

7. VII

1. Corsica
2. Seneca himself was of Spanish extraction.

10. X

1. Qu. oysters from Britain.
2. The allusion is evidently to Regulus.

16. XVI

1. I think Madvig's *ademisset* spoils the sense. *Dedisset* means: "when you bid me mourn the loss of the Gracchi you bid me blame fortune for having given me such sons." "'Tis better to have loved and lost than to have never loved at all." —J. E. B. M.

19. XIX

1. Alcestis-
2. The context shows that *sanctitas* is opposed to "rapacity," "taking bribes," like the Celaeno of Juvenal viii. —J. E. B. M.

1. I

1. See Merivale's *History of the Romans Under the Empire*, Chapter XIV.

3. III

1. If it is a pain to dwell upon the thought of lost friends, of course you do not continually refresh the memory of them by speaking of them.

5. V

1. See my note on *invidiam facere alicui* in Juvenal 15. —J. E. B. Mayor. *Dead Souls*. (Translator's note.)

7. VII

1. Koch declares that this cannot be the true reading, and suggests *deminutio*, "degradation."

13. XIII

1. This seems to have been part of the ceremony of dedication. Pulvillus was dedicating the Temple of Jupiter in the Capitol. See Livy, II, 8; Cicero, *Pro Domo*, paragraph cxxi.
2. Lucius Æmilius Paullus conquered Perses, the last King of Macedonia, BC 168.
3. "For he had four sons, two, as has been already related, adopted into other families, Scipio and Fabius; and two others, who were still children, by his second wife, who lived in his own house. Of these, one died five days before Æmilius's triumph, at the age of fourteen, and the other, twelve years old, died three days after it: so that there was no Roman that did not grieve for him," etc.
   —*Plutarch,* Life of Æmilius, *Chapter XXXV*

14. XIV

1. AUC 695, BC 59

17. XVII

1. Virgil, *Aeneid*, III, 418.
2. See Mayor's note on Juvenal I, and above, Chapter 16, §4

19. XIX

1. Lipsius points out that this idea is borrowed from the comic poet Antiphanes. See Meineke's *Comic Fragments*, p. 3.

22. XXII

1. This I believe to be the meaning of the text, but Koch reasonably conjectures that the true reading is *editur subscriptio*, "an indictment was made out against him." See *On Benefits*, Book III, Chapter 26.

26. XXVI

1. *Ruinae*; Koch's *urinae* is a misprint.